if you're

clueless

about

retirement

planning

and

want to

know more

by SETH GODIN

Dearborn
Financial Publishing, Inc.®

If You're Clueless about Retirement Planning and Want to Know More

Executive Editor: Cynthia A. Zigmund
Managing Editor: Jack Kiburz
Interior and Cover Design: Karen Engelmann

© 1997 by Seth Godin Productions, Inc.

Published by Dearborn Financial Publishing, Inc.®

Printed in the United States of America

97 98 99 10 9 8 7 6 5 4 3 2 1

Library of Congress Cataloging-in-Publication Data
Godin, Seth.
    If you're clueless about retirement planning and want to know more / Seth Godin.
        p.   cm.
    Includes index.
    ISBN 0-7931-2553-7 (paper)
      1. Retirement Income--United States--Planning.   2. Investments--United States.
    3. Finance, Personal--United States.   I. Title.
    HG179.G635   1997
    332.024'01--dc21   97-5607
                                                        CIP

Acknowledgments

Thanks to Jack Kiburz and Cindy Zigmund at Dearborn, whose editorial guidance made this book possible. Karen Watts was the driving force behind the Clueless concept, and Lynn Adkins did an expert job of pulling it all together.

Thanks to Robin Dellabough, Lisa DiMona, Nana Sledzieski, Leslie Sharpe, Susan Kushnick, Lisa Lindsay, Julie Maner, and Sarah Silbert at SGP for their never-ending insight and hard work. And kudos to Sidney Short for his layout work, Nikki Coddington and Gwen Bronson for their copyediting talent, and Vicki Fischer for her proofreading skills.

Contents

Chapter One: Getting a Clue about Retirement Planning   1

Chapter Two: Write the Script for Your Retirement   19

Chapter Three: Taking Care of Numero Uno   31

Chapter Four: Climb to the Top of the Investment Tower   45

Chapter Five: Uncle Sam and Your Retirement Plans   59

Chapter Six: The Three Amigos in Your Pocket   73

Chapter Seven: How the 401(k) Plan Works 4-U   85

Chapter Eight: Diversify, Diversify, and Diversify Some More!   97

Chapter Nine: A Cast of Thousands Working for You   113

Chapter Ten: Fine-Tune Your Retirement Plan   125

Chapter Eleven: Now, Back to the Future   135

Chapter Twelve: You Can Leverage
Your Way through Cyberspace   155

Chapter Thirteen: That's a Wrap!   165

Glossary   168

Resources   176

Index   182

GETTING
a clue
about
retirement
PLANNING

CHAPTER ONE

*Planning for retirement is about giving yourself what you deserve and **taking control** of your future even though you may feel you have no control over your present. Getting the **clues** you need to put a swell retirement plan in place is a lot **easier** than you think.*

If you're like most people, you're busy working to make this life the best it can possibly be for yourself and your family. It probably takes about all the energy you have to get it together here and now. It's hard enough to plan for next year, or even next week, and thinking about retirement can seem totally overwhelming, especially if you're clueless about where to start. But if you're reading this, you already have a jump start on most people because you're showing some interest in the subject. That is the biggest and most important step to take. So congratulate yourself. You're smarter and more responsible than you give yourself credit for when it comes to planning for your future. You have overcome a giant hurdle.

Actually, planning for retirement is a lot easier than you think. It all comes down to a few basic ideas and simple steps to create a plan that works for you. You need to:

1. Set aside money—not a lot, but some—on a regular basis.

2. Plop the money into a plan that was designed to encourage you to save for your retirement. That means an Individual Retirement Account (IRA); a company-sponsored plan, such as a 401(k); or a Keogh, which is a plan self-employed people can establish for themselves. Your money will grow free from taxes until you retire, at which point that money will probably be taxed at a much lower rate.

3. Invest the money that is sitting in your retirement plan. Pick exactly which investment companies will manage your money and which investment options are best for you.

The point is that you can start simply. As you become more comfortable doing the retirement planning three-step dance, you may want to add some fancy, more sophisticated moves. But you don't have to do that. You can stick with a simple plan and still get where you want to go.

The Good News

You don't need $10,000 or $5,000 to start. You don't even need $1,000. You don't need to hire a financial planner or investment adviser. You don't need a calculator and you don't need to rummage through the storage bin to locate your advanced algebra textbook. Planning for retirement is not about mathematical investment equations.

Planning for retirement is about giving yourself what you deserve. It's about taking control of your future even though you may feel as if you have no control over your present. It's about knowing what your options are and then choosing the ones that work for you. These aren't set in stone—you can be flexible and always alter your plans further down the road if you need to. The important thing is to start building a structure that can be modified as you go along.

The good news is that planning for retirement is one of the few areas of your life where you really are in charge. It's an opportunity for you to think about what you really want and where you want to go, and then plot a course to get there. Creating a better future—distant as that future may seem now—is a second chance to realize your dreams.

You've Probably Already Started

If you have worked, and your employer has truncated your paycheck for something called FICA, you have already begun contributing to Social Security, a forced plan for retirement. FICA stands for the Federal Insurance Contributions Act, which mandates that employees participate in this plan. It may not be much, but it is something.

Predicting the death of Social Security has become commonplace. A recent poll of Americans in their twenties and thirties, for example, found that Generation Xers are more likely to believe in the existence of UFOs than they are that Social Security will be around when they're ready to retire. The reality is that you can take with a grain of salt the scary headlines and the political naysayers who tell you Social Security is on the verge of bankruptcy. It's calming to remember that sensational news stories sell more newspapers and magazines, and politicians sometimes preach doom and gloom to cloud their own sorry performances in office.

Social Security will probably survive. In 1983, Democrats and Republicans put aside their

THE PIGGY BANK METHOD

You'd be surprised how much you can save by throwing small amounts of money into a piggy bank. Just make sure you have one that is difficult to get into. Here's what you can put into the bank:

• **Loose change** at the end of every day. Just 45¢ a day turns into over $160 a year.

• The money you saved **renting** a $3 movie for two instead of spending full price for each of you at the theater.

• The **$5.00** you loaned a friend. If you had enough to lend yesterday, you won't miss it when it's repaid into your piggy bank today.

After six months, open the little porcelain porker. You'll be amazed at the size of your no-risk, no-pain investment. Take your dimes and quarters and dollars, put them into your checking account, and immediately write a check to yourself to deposit in the tax-deferred retirement account you have started.

THE CLUELESS MAJORITY

If you feel clueless about retirement, you are not alone. A whopping 82 percent of all adult Americans are "financially illiterate," according to a survey conducted by the Investor Protection Trust, a nonprofit organization in Arlington, Virginia.

The reason for this high illiteracy rate is a lack of education on the subject. High-school graduates are capable of calculating the area of a circle, and people with college degrees can provide seven different reasons why Hamlet dithered. But academic schools don't do a great job of preparing students for real life. Getting the financial equations for your retirement entails formulas that are a lot more practical—and easier, too. And determining a course of action will be a lot smoother and safer for you than it was for Hamlet who waited so long to decide what to be that he was forced by someone else not to be.

partisan squabbling to reconfigure the plan so that it will work well into the first quarter of the next century. And chances are Congress will administer another dose of financially responsible medicine for the years beyond.

Politicians on both sides of the aisle are suggesting measures to ensure the financial health of Social Security well into the twenty-first century. Some proposals would allow people who pay into Social Security the opportunity to invest their own FICA contributions in stocks and bonds and mutual funds, for example. Of course, any revamping of Social Security will take some time, but the political will does appear to exist to make the program financially sound for years to come.

Unfortunately, Social Security most likely will not provide you with all the money you need for retirement. For instance, by the time you retire, it might cover only your monthly housing expense or your grocery and utilities bills. To enjoy your retirement, you'll need other funds and assets. The goal of this book is to show you how to achieve these goals and how you can use them to build a sound plan for a secure future.

This Is Not Your Parents' Retirement

Right now, talking about Social Security may seem as remote as the planet Pluto, and a little disconcerting, to boot. Indeed, your images of the retirees who receive those government-issued checks may be so far removed from your mental

Qualifying for Social Security

You are entitled to receive Social Security if you have worked 40 quarters (quarters of a year) in your lifetime, or a total of ten years. And, even though you may have worked less than ten years, you still may have accumulated the magic 40 quarters. That's because Social Security has its own method for calculating quarters of a year. In Social Security mathematics, a quarter is equivalent to a specific amount of money earned each year. In 1996, $640 in earnings was equal to one Social Security quarter.

Thus, those summer or part-time jobs you took years ago may be tallied in your Social Security quarterly account. For instance, if you earned $640 in 1996, Social Security credited you with one quarter of work even though you earned that money during only six weeks of work. A total of $1,280 in 1996 earnings translates into two Social Security quarters, but no matter how much you earn a year, you can accumulate only four quarters in any one year. Given this way of calculating quarters, you may well have 40 in the Social Security bank.

Every year or so, the government changes the earnings baseline equivalent to a quarter. To check how many quarters Social Security has credited to your account, call (800) 772-1213. Remember to have your Social Security number ready when you make the call. And may the quarters be with you.

picture of yourself, it might seem as if they *were* from another planet. Not me, you say. I'm not going to struggle now to spend my retirement playing shuffleboard with Jerry Seinfeld's parents in Clearwater, Florida.

That doesn't have to be your retirement. Your generation will dictate what retirement in the twenty-first century will be. You can make your retirement anything you want. The reason to take control of your future is to enjoy it. And the fact is, you can expect your life to be longer and much healthier than your parents' or grandparents' lives.

Retirement does not have to be a separate chapter in your life. Think of it as a passage from one lifestyle to another, a time for you to apply and relish the experiences and knowledge you have acquired. Add money to that hard-won knowledge and you'll have the formula for adventure and your own brand of fun. Retirement planning is a way to make sure the pleasure principle is a reality for you for your entire life.

It Seems Daunting, but It's Really a No-Brainer

Taking control of your plans for retirement is like doing your laundry. It's not hard, but you have to do it and do it regularly. That means making routine contributions to your retirement savings plan.

Procrastinating about the laundry and procrastinating about retirement planning present similar problems. You know the longer you let the laundry pile up, the fewer clothes you have to wear because most of your stuff is smelly or dirty or both. It's also heavier to lug to the laundry room. So it is with retirement planning. The more you delay saving for the future, the fewer options you will have for the way you'll want to spend those retirement years and, worse still, the more difficult it will be to amass the necessary assets.

Once you get accustomed to saving and investing for retirement, you can add a few simple bells and whistles. Like separating the laundry whites from the darks and the machine washables from delicate hand-washed fabrics, you will learn to make distinctions between the types of investments you make for retirement.

For instance, you will want some fixed-income investments such as bonds and some equity investments such as stocks. Among equities, you will want some growth stocks, which can further be divided between aggressive growth stocks (these are usually found among small but fast-growing firms) and regular growth stocks (these are usually the medium-size firms with a good track record plus in-demand products or services).

Just Do It!

You may feel that building a foundation for your retirement is totally out of your reach. Like so many people, you probably are struggling today just to pay for your immediate needs. Most of your paycheck may go toward paying down loans, paying off bills, and saving a little for a modest three-day outing with your friends or family. How in the world can you expect to save for the distant future?

Worse still, investment gurus concoct financial equations that are downright frightening. They tell you that you'll need umpteen zillions of dollars or the equivalent of the value of a small island resort by the time you retire in order to live the lifestyle you want.

Forget those stratospheric numbers. Your goal is not some specific amount of money you want to amass by a certain date. Those mathematical monsters are nothing more than a retirement nightmare on Elm Street. So, wake up.

All you need to do is to get a retirement plan started and to make regular contributions. A modest but regular savings plan—begun before you are 40 years old—can absolutely blossom by the time you want to retire. So focus on those three basic steps for forging your retirement plan:

1. Set aside money.

2. Plop the money into a plan designed to encourage you to save for your retirement.

3. Invest the money that is sitting in your retirement plan.

Your Spending I.Q.

 If you spend your money foolishly, you have less to invest wisely. The following questions will give you a yardstick to determine your spending smarts. Select the response which best reflects your situation and mark the appropriate response number next to each question.

1) Totally like me   4) Only a little like me
2) A lot like me   5) Not at all like me
3) Equally like and unlike me

_____ I deposit my paycheck into an account each pay period.

_____ I save each paycheck stub indicating earnings, deductions, taxes, savings, and so on.

_____ I set aside a portion of my earnings each pay period to cover fixed expenses.

_____ I contribute to a tax-deferred retirement savings account on a regular schedule.

_____ My spending is managed according to a written budget.

_____ Grocery spending is planned in advance with a list, and purchases are made primarily from that list.

_____ I/we rarely make more than one trip a week to the grocery store.

_____ Grocery and other coupons are used whenever possible.

_____ I comparison shop for quality, value, and price for practically every purchase, big or small.

_____ I pay the entire balance on my credit cards.

____ I do not have any loans (excluding first mortgage and one auto) with a balance owed.

____ I have comparison shopped for auto insurance within the last year.

____ I dine out no more than once a week.

____ At the end of the day, I can account for all the cash I have spent.

____ I balance my checking account with each statement.

Now, tally the numbers and see how you score.

15–21: Superior. You've got the credentials to give others advice on spending wisely.

22–34: Pretty Good. Concentrate on those areas where you are weak.

35–49: Average. You need to devise ways to improve your spending so you'll have more to save for your retirement.

50–64: Lousy. You need to immediately change your spending pattern if you want to avoid major financial headaches.

65 or more: Terrible. This book will be a major help.

You can get additional assistance by sending a self-addressed stamped envelope to: National Center for Financial Education, P.O. Box 43070, San Diego, CA 92163. Request these pamphlets: "Spending by Choice," "Dealing with Creditors," "How to Get Out of Debt," and "How to Develop a Spending Plan."

What...Me Worry?

The alternative to taking control of your own retirement planning is to just do nothing and hope that someone else will take care of you. Such pipe dreams may be pleasant, but there is no substitute for relying on your own efforts to formulate a retirement plan. You're on your own here, because the reality is there are a lot of people who won't be able to help:

- Don't count on your parents to leave you a bundle of money even if their current assets seem more than ample. The older your parents get, the more money they are likely to need for a small army of helpers to care for the lawn, shovel the snow, clean the house, and fix a meal or two, if they remain in their own home. Even more expensive are nursing homes and those extended-care facilities that provide a small apartment, a communal meal or two every day, and round-the-clock medical staff.

- Don't count on your employer to provide you with a guaranteed income and medical insurance for all your retirement years. Fewer and fewer companies are providing monthly pensions based on a percentage of your salary in the last couple years of your employment. Corporate downsizing and employee job-hopping have made even fewer people eligible for pensions that provide a specific amount of money every month of every retirement year. As for employer-paid medical coverage after an employee retires, that is rare, indeed, these days.

- Don't count on the government for the money to enjoy retirement. Social Security will help to pay some of your bills, but you'll need other financial resources to be comfortable, have fun, and feel financially secure.

- Don't count on beating the odds. The odds of winning $1 million in the lottery are less than one million to one.

The odds are even worse that you will:

- Discover a signed Rembrandt canvas at the flea market

- Meet a Hollywood producer willing to pay you a million dollars for that fabulous movie idea of yours

- Get rewarded with a seven-figure bonus for that marketing plan you designed

Of course, if huge amounts of money should unexpectedly come your way, you will have the financial resources to get somebody else to buy this book and read it to you at your leisure. But since this likelihood is very small, you need to take command now of your plan for the future. The advantage to this, though, is that you have the power to make it happen the way you want it to. You also have the luxury to think about what you want and how to get there—with lots of time to be flexible about changing your course of action if you need to. Your retirement is your responsibility—and you're in charge.

It's a Plan, Not a Prison

Once you realize how simple it is to create a retirement plan, you may be tempted to make it too detailed and complicated. Don't make the mistake of becoming entangled in the myriad, and sometimes esoteric, choices available to you. The simpler the plan, the easier it is to mold and rearrange. Don't overengineer your retirement plan so it becomes a prison.

For instance, let's say you want to open an IRA at a brokerage firm. Ideally, you will want to look for a firm that:

- Charges a low fee to open your plan

- Charges a low annual fee to maintain your plan

- Provides easy-to-understand statements concerning the investments in your plan

DID YOU KNOW?

If you save **$2,000** every year for ten years beginning when you are 25 years old and ending when you are 35, that $20,000 placed in a tax-deferred retirement plan could potentially equal $250,000 when you are 65 years old. The magic of making $20,000 equal **$250,000** is called compounding, which you'll learn about in chapter four.

Retirement Myths

A recent congressional study found that half of all people enter their retirement with less than $10,000 in savings, possibly with the mistaken belief that it will be sufficient to carry them through. Let's look at some of the myths that contribute to this sort of retirement mismanagement so that your dream for tomorrow is not scuttled on the rocks of misconceptions.

Social Security Will Take Care of You. Social Security will probably be there for you, but that government check will not cover all your monthly retirement expenses. If you are married and your combined income is between $50,000 and $100,000 a year, Social Security will provide less than 20 percent of your preretirement income. The average monthly benefit for a couple, both of whom are receiving benefits, is $1,140 a month. How far will that sum take you? Probably no further than your local convenience store.

Your Retirement Will Be Short. People who reach age 65 can expect to live another 18 years or more. Forced or early retirement might mean you will be retired nearly as long as you have worked. It takes a lot of money to fund all your retirement years.

Your Retirement Expenses Will Be Lower Than Your Preretirement Spending. Barely. A rule of thumb is that your retirement expenses will run 80 percent of your preretirement spending. If you and your spouse have a combined income during your working years of $80,000, the formula suggests you'll need $64,000 a year in order to maintain your current lifestyle. Multiply that by 20 years of retirement and you are talking serious money.

Your Parents Will Leave You Their Money. Think again. Your parents are probably facing the same challenge now that you will later. They're trying to stretch their dollars over many years. They may deplete most of their money before it goes to you. Worse still, you may need to financially support your parents just at the time you are ready to retire.

You Can Start Saving When You're Older. Sure, and you can start training for the Olympics when you are 40 years old. But look at the numbers. For every ten years you delay starting to save for retirement, you will need to save more than twice as much to build a nest egg the same size. Take a look at the high cost of delay. Assume your savings are invested at 8 percent in a tax-deferred account. To amass $500,000 by age 65, you will need to:

Save per Month	Beginning at Age
$144	25
336	35
849	45
2,734	55

- Offers low or no fees to switch from one investment to another

- Offers lots of different investments from which to choose

Comparing all these options from among the scores of brokerage firms could consume every "free" weekend hour for a year. Better to make a decision NOW based on the scope of investments offered, for instance, and then fine-tune the fee considerations later.

You can do this later by letting the brokerage firm know that you are aware of other firms with lower fees. The firm might match the competition. If not, you can always switch your IRA investments to another firm.

The important thing is to take some action now. If you wait six months or a year to make a decision, you may be tempted to spend the money you could have invested. You also will have "lost" the money your money could have earned had it been invested.

It is not necessary to study and understand all the information and options available to you. Trying to do that will not only confuse you, but can discourage you from adhering to your overall goal: to have the investments and assets you need for the retirement you want.

You also cannot plan for every eventuality in your life, so don't try to design a retirement plan for 14 different scenarios. You don't walk out the door with a hundred pounds of clothes and necessities for subzero weather and 110° afternoons alike, for hailstorms and ice storms, for hurricanes and earthquakes. You wouldn't get far carrying baggage for every climatic possibility. Instead, you dress for the current forecast. You may get drenched by a sudden rainstorm, but at least your burden is light enough to allow you to scurry for cover.

The same holds for retirement planning. Don't overload your retirement plan to cushion yourself against every possible thing that could happen. Just as preposterously great things will probably not fall in your lap, you can be pretty confident that every possible disaster will not befall you at the same time. Chances are that your employer will not abscond with your retirement savings during the week that all your stock market investments lose half their value, your home insurance firm goes bankrupt as you watch your house burn down, and you contract a rare disease not covered by your health insurance. Don't waste your time worrying about trying to remedy every potential hazard.

The beauty of a sensible retirement plan is that you have the power to make it happen any way you want it to. And if you start early enough, you have the luxury to think about what you want and how to get there—with lots of time to be flexible about changing your course of action if you need to. Just create a basic but effective plan and be ready to adapt it to meet changing circumstances. Your retirement is your future—and you're in charge.

What You'll Learn

In this book, you'll discover how to steer through the basic concepts of planning for retirement and what steps to take to secure the financial future you want for yourself and your family. You will learn:

- How to write the screenplay for the retirement movie in which you star (chapter two)

- How to save without pain and discover the big bonus you get for saving sooner rather than later (chapter three)

- The various types of investments for retirement plans (chapter four)

- The type of plans available to you and how to get the most from these plans (chapter five)

- The three basic principles for investing in a retirement plan (chapter six)

- The ins and outs of 401(k) plans, the most popular retirement savings plans (chapter seven)

- How to diversify your retirement plan by investing in real estate and insurance (chapter eight)

- How to find the people and institutions to help you plan, establish, and maintain your retirement plan (chapter nine)

- How to fine-tune your plan (chapter ten)

- How to determine how much money you will need to retire (chapter eleven)

- How to use cyberspace to plan your retirement (chapter twelve)

- How to create a legacy for yourself (chapter thirteen)

- How to find the resources you need to further explore retirement planning (resources)

Sprinkled throughout the book are tips on how to save and invest, quizzes on spending and risk, and fraud-buster moves you can make to ensure your plan is safe and secure.

Keep the Faith...in Yourself

Experience has shown you that even your simplest plan can get flummoxed. But, life does go on and so do you. A canceled flight might delay your departure for a holiday, but it rarely cancels out your entire vacation. A sprained ankle may inconvenience you for a time, but it doesn't make you permanently disabled. Mistakenly putting your favorite wool sweater into the dryer may shrink it to toddler proportions, but does not destroy your entire wardrobe.

FACTOID

Life expectancy is rising. That means you'll spend almost one-third of your life in retirement. You need to plan for those years so you'll have the money to enjoy all that free time.

The same is true with retirement planning. Setbacks may occur. You may find that you have invested in a certain mutual fund one year, only to see the value of those shares decline 70 percent the next year. You may discover that your bank is charging three times the amount to maintain your retirement plan as the bank across the street. You may realize you forgot to pay your rent last week and now don't have the money to make your regular contribution to your retirement plan.

Don't let those mishaps and missteps—whether they're of your making or someone else's—keep you from pursuing your long-term goals. You know how to handle and overcome unforeseen obstacles in other parts of your life. You probably get frustrated or angry or both, but you carry on, knowing that one bad experience certainly will not deter you from getting what you want.

Apply that confidence to your retirement planning. Know-it-alls may gloat over mistakes you make, but such unsolicited comments need not waylay you from your overall plan. Those critics just might be dispensing retirement wisdom to deflect attention from the lack of any plans they have made for themselves.

Have faith in yourself to overcome unforeseen obstacles. The righteous stuff you need to create a successful retirement is confidence and determination. This book will fill in the rest.

Spending Costs You More Than You Think

The penalty for spending rather than saving and investing is huge, particularly when you are young. Take a look at what spending less and investing the savings can mean to you. Assume you are getting an 8 percent rate of return on your investments and that you put them in a tax-deferred account. Look at how much you will have at age 65 if you save and invest rather than spend even as little as $50 a month.

Save & invest $50 a month at age	You'll have at age 65
25	$162,093
35	70,882
45	28,633
55	9,064

Save & invest $75 a month at age	You'll have at age 65
25	$243,140
35	106,322
45	43,950
55	13,596

Save & invest $100 a month at age	You'll have at age 65
25	$324,186
35	141,763
45	57,266
55	18,128

Save & invest $150 a month at age	You'll have at age 65
25	$486,279
35	212,645
45	86,900
55	27,193

WRITE *the* script *for your* RETIREMENT

Your retirement planning starts in your right brain where your imagination and creativity reside. Use those talents to write your own retirement screenplay. You get to **star** in the production, design the sets, and **direct the movie.**

Does thinking about retirement planning make your stomach muscles tense, your palms sweaty, and your throat dry? If you feel intimidated and overwhelmed by the challenge of analyzing and studying investment parameters, rates of return, defined-contribution plans, and tax-deferred vehicles, you're not alone.

But there's no reason to have an anxiety attack over this. You have the smarts, you are filled with ideas, and your creativity abounds. Recall the endorphin high you get when your imagination starts pumping. You feel great. You feel potent. The current obstacles in your life crumble, making way for fabulous future possibilities.

This is your opportunity to let these powerful parts of yourself run rampant. You don't need your left brain to get started on your retirement plan. So turn it off. At this point in your retirement planning, it is not necessary to address the principles of investing or to sift through the different types of retirement plans available. You certainly don't need to calculate how much you will need when you are 65 years old. Not now.

Now is the time to take the padlock off your imagination and those awesome creative talents you possess. Turn on your right brain. Imagination and creativity are the keys you need to get started on a retirement plan. So, let them rip, roar, and surge to tsunamic proportions and produce a vision of your future retirement.

RETIREMENT LIFESTYLE

Five things you could be doing in retirement:

• More of the **leisure** activities you enjoy now.

• **Volunteer** work at something you really care about.

• Living someplace you've always **dreamed** of.

• Spending more **time** with your friends and family.

• Taking a **course** or lessons that your current schedule just does not allow.

Accentuate the Positive

You were born in the twentieth century, but the twenty-first century will mark your most productive years and your greatest achievements. It also will be the century in which you enjoy your retirement years.

Each generation has the right to its own vision of retirement and to transform that vision into a reality. Shaping a positive image of retirement will help to motivate and stimulate you to put together a solid plan. And once you have a concrete script, you can refer to it often to help relieve any anxieties you may have about your future.

The screenplay of your retirement will change as you grow older. Marriage will put a spouse in the picture. Children and grandchildren may be added. Conversely, divorce might eliminate someone from the story line.

As your horizons broaden and your experiences deepen, you may adjust the plans for your retirement lifestyle. That's merely an indication that you are emotionally healthy and intellectually with-it.

Get an Attitude

It's up to you to get a healthy attitude about your retirement. You can create your own positive image of your retirement or you can let negative models from the past constrain you. Just take a look at the difference in attitudes about retirement taken by the Star Trek captains of the *USS Enterprise.*

For James T. Kirk, retirement meant obsolescence in some distant quadrant of the universe, where younger generations of Starfleet officers might cordially pay a visit but secretly snicker at his pitiful existence before propelling at warp speed to more fascinating worlds and experiences. Burdened with such a prospect, Kirk always seemed a bit too combative to relish the few times he was not getting into or out of some galactic mess.

Contrast that with the Next Generation's Captain Jean-Luc Picard. He broke the old molds and looked forward to a retirement zipping from one galaxy to another in search of archaeological artifacts, stopping only long enough for a little horseback riding and a taste or two of fine wine. His primary concern was that he would not know when to give up the bridge and pursue his retirement plan. Meanwhile, Picard managed to maintain his cool in crisis after crisis and relax in between.

Those two distinct visions of retirement might explain why Kirk's anxiety level day to day often bordered on the neurotic and why Picard always seemed more mellow and in control of himself. Picard looked forward to discovering relics of the past; Kirk worried about being a relic of the past.

High Cost of Delayed Savings

 **The sooner you start saving, the less you need to save each year prior to retirement. Take a look at the high cost of procrastinating.**

Let's say you want to save $200,000 by the time you retire at age 60. Based on an 8 percent return on your investment savings, here's what you'll need to invest. Notice that the longer you delay, the more you'll need to save each year.

Age	Years to Retirement	Yearly Savings to Reach $200,000
40	20 years	$4,400
45	15 years	7,400
50	10 years	13,800
55	5 years	34,100

Save early and as much as you can. Playing catch-up is no fun. It's a lifestyle backbreaker.

The Dollars and Cents You'll Need Tomorrow to Equal One Dollar Today

Years from Today	Inflation Rate			
	3%	4%	5%	6%
5	$1.16	$1.22	$1.28	$1.34
10	1.34	1.48	1.63	1.79
15	1.56	1.80	2.08	2.40
20	1.81	2.19	2.65	3.21
25	2.09	2.67	3.39	4.29

Delete 20 Centuries

Before you can create your own image of retirement for the new millennium, you need to chuck the outmoded models of the past 20 centuries. That should be fairly easy because the concept of retirement just didn't exist for most people for most of recorded history. People were born, started working in adolescence, and then continued a life of drudgery until they dropped dead. Think about peasants in medieval France, or even Grandma and Grandpa Walton, and you've got the picture.

That toil-to-the death model gave way to one that was possibly even less attractive. In the next historical version of retirement, frail, elderly folk were relegated to a chair in one corner of the back parlor as the rest of the family went about the business of living.

The possibility of a slightly more active and independent retirement emerged when pension plans and Social Security payments provided enough money for those over the age of 65 to retire to a modest Florida bungalow or even to take a once-in-a-life-time, 14-day tour of Europe. Between visits from the children and grandchildren, these old folks played endless hours of bridge or gin rummy. They died suddenly and alone in their homes or spent the last few months of life in a nursing facility.

The parents of the very oldest baby boomers populate the current image of retirement. Fit and well-groomed in V-necked sweaters, these people play golf and tennis in a country-club setting somewhere in Arizona or North Carolina. Their homes are neat, clean, and tastefully decorated. They shop in upscale department and specialty stores where they pay the retail price for the birthday gifts they bestow upon their children and grandchildren. The most adventuresome take medieval history courses at a university in Limerick, Ireland or spend three months with a volunteer program in Budapest teaching Hungarians how to speak English. With ample savings, the very old buy into an extended-care facility which will also provide nursing home services as they grow even older and more frail.

That polite, well-ordered generation—the members of which are proud of their ability to take care of themselves—will be succeeded by the baby boomers who, according to numerous surveys, have been appallingly lax in planning for their retirement years. They have spent their way into a corner framed by one wall of huge debts and the other wall of few savings. How they will manage their retirement remains a mystery. Perhaps they will attempt to make genteel poverty a virtue. Or, as they have done in the past with other things, maybe they'll convince themselves that their mangled finances are a metaphor for the state of the world.

The Vision Thing: Zen into the Next Millennium

Those retirement models of years past will not be yours. You can't replicate the retirement of your parents or grandparents. That would not serve your best interests.

Certainly, you don't want to use the model of the baby boomers who have procrastinated themselves into a real mess.

Begin with the "vision thing." A nearsighted approach to retirement planning can keep you from your long-term aspirations because you'll never put together a plan today if you can't see something good for yourself tomorrow.

Try a little Zen and engage in some creative visualization of your retirement in the next century. What would you like to do if you weren't doing what you are doing now? Picture yourself in a place, doing—or maybe just being—something. Let the tape of your retirement run for a while.

Stare at the space below for Your Retirement Visualization Exercise.

THE REAL ESTATE MYTH

Myth: My home will provide the bulk of assets I need for retirement.

Reality: Sure, the value of your house or condo will probably increase and you can sell your property for a tidy profit when you retire. But you will probably need to use some of those profits for another place to live. Only some of the money can be used to buy groceries and pay for your entertainment. To completely cover all of your retirement expenses, you'll need to make some investments outside your home.

Who Says Money Doesn't Buy Happiness?

Whatever your vision of retirement, unless you're retiring to the Mosquito Coast, you will need money.

That money will buy you the necessities—a roof over your head, bread on the table, and threads on your body—with enough left over to do things like meander through cyberspace, travel to see your family and friends, and entertain yourself.

While gobs of money won't buy complete happiness, a comfortable bank account will make the good times even better. Money doesn't guarantee good health, but it does let you pay for the visits to the doctors' offices that help prevent bad health. Money doesn't buy friends, but it does pay for the plane ticket to visit them. And, of course, money does not buy love, but it does let you take care of yourself so those you love don't have to do it for you.

Money does matter. The more money you have when you retire, the greater freedom you'll enjoy.

A Dollar Today, Cents Tomorrow

You've heard the tales from your grandparents about their parents—how they worked 40 hours a week for only $60, but still managed to save money for their first home. Sounds amazing. Of course, a soft drink back then cost only a dime, and that first home cost less than $10,000, about three times their salary.

The wisdom of those stories lies not in how hard they worked, but in how the value of one dollar

THE GIFT THAT KEEPS ON GIVING

Tired of getting stupid gifts from your parents and relatives that you'll never use or wear? Why not tell them you'd like a **U.S. savings bond?** It's easy for them to buy, and they are sure to be impressed with how responsible you are. Better still, that U.S. savings bond will increase in value. That's probably not going to happen with those gold-leaf appetizer plates you got from Aunt Martha. Twenty years from now, if you still have them, they'll just be taking up space and collecting dust balls.

decreased over time. Inflation is definitely something you must factor into your plan for retirement. You will need more money 30 years from now than you need today just to buy the same groceries, fill the tank of the car, and pay for a place to live.

The inflation rate changes month to month and year to year. During the 1950s and 1960s, it was about what it is today. Inflation soared to over 12 percent during the late 1970s, but fortunately, has gradually fallen to approximately 3 to 4 percent in the mid–1990s. Even at this relatively low level, inflation will eat the value of your retirement dollars.

The Silent Thief

It's tempting to ignore the silent thief of inflation today because the rate hunches at below 4 percent. But that low rate can be deceiving.

Look at what this means for your spending. Let's say you and your spouse go out for dinner to celebrate your tenth wedding anniversary. With wine, the check comes to $60. You hand the waiter two crisp $50 bills—you don't charge it, of course—and you get back $40. You leave the waiter a 15 percent tip of $9 for a total tab of $69.

Ten years pass in which inflation has risen by 4 percent a year. Still married, the two of you return to the same restaurant and order the same meal you ordered ten years earlier. At the end of the meal, you give the waiter a crisp $100 bill. This time, the price has risen and the bill comes to $88.80. The waiter returns $11.20 to you. A 15 percent tip on the $88.80 comes to $13.30—that's $2.10 more than you have. Oops. You hope your spouse has it.

Ignoring inflation can create much bigger problems than scrounging for a tip. For instance, your spouse's $100,000 insurance policy may provide adequate financial security for you today, but at a 4 percent inflation rate, that $100,000 will buy only $67,000 worth of goods ten years from now. After 20 years, that $100,000 will buy $44,000 of food, clothes, and shelter.

Don't let the silent thief of inflation rob you blind. Save today and invest so you can keep ahead of the inflation you and your family will face.

Invest to Combat Inflation

How can you save enough money to counter inflation? You probably can't if all you do is squirrel your money into an empty videocassette box or stash it in the drawer behind your turtleneck sweaters.

What you can do is make your savings increase in value at least as fast as—or even faster than—inflation. That means investing your savings into stocks, bonds, or real estate so your money will earn more money.

Stretch Your Dollars

There are some things you can do now, that won't cost you a bundle of money, but that can make the money you save for retirement go even further. You already have a treasure trove of some of the important things you'll need 30 or 40 years from now.

For instance, if you've never smoked or have beaten the nicotine habit, your health insurance costs during retirement will be less than a smoker's. Moreover, you'll be in better physical shape to enjoy your retirement.

Cultivating an ability to enjoy life without spending a whole lot of money is another good investment. Would you rather spend an evening talking with friends over pizza, or would you prefer to fork over $100 to see a basketball playoff game alone? If you opted for the expensive solitary outing, you'll need a lot more money in retirement than if you can get a high from relationships.

Spend, Spend, Spend...Time with Your Friends

Spending time with your friends and family is a good investment. Spending money now on a lot of things is not. If you aren't convinced, answer this question: Can you recall all the birthday gifts you received each of the past 15 years? Probably not. But it's a good bet that you can recall more than a few memories of the time you spent, and the things you did, with your friends and family on those birthdays.

A HANGOVER FROM 200 PROOF GREED

The savings and loan crisis in the early 1990s was a hangover from the greed of the 1980s. More specifically, greedy politicians, who were pampered by greedy bankers, created a house of cards that came crashing down when the economy and financial markets cooled in the early '90s.

A combination of factors led to a dismal situation: Industry regulators didn't have enough staff or funding to monitor thrift banks. States adopted liberal rules for the thrifts, and the federal government insured all deposits.

When the thrift deposit insurance system became strained beyond its capacity, all efforts to regulate the assault on the taxpayer-funded insurance system were defeated. So when the final bill came due, it was left to the taxpayers to bail-out—to the tune of a half trillion dollars.

Even if you lose a few gray cells of memory in your old age, you will still be able to recall the moments you've shared with others a lot more quickly and clearly than the things you've bought in the past.

Hobbies and Collectibles

No book on retirement planning would be complete without a few words on hobbies. You've heard people contend, "My hobbies will keep me busy in retirement." Don't believe it. You may like to dry flowers and arrange them, or fiddle with the layout of your electric trains, or collect Fred Flintstone paraphernalia.

That's fine and dandy. Just don't kid yourself that you'll want to engage in those hobbies all day long, seven days, or even three days, a week every year of your retirement. You'll need and want to do some other things. You'll want time outside your hobby or hobbies to see a movie, do some volunteer work, and to take out-of-town trips to visit friends and family.

Even your hobbies will entail some spending. Your garden may not supply enough flowers, the trains will need to be repaired, and you may need an extra bedroom just for Fred and Wilma. All that will take money.

Collecting on Those Collectibles...Not!

Collectibles as a retirement investment sits very high on the list of self-delusions. There's no guarantee those collectibles will be worth any more in 40 years than they are today. Think about it. You probably are not the only one who has saved the first-generation video game of the Teenage Mutant Ninja Turtles.

Adding to your collectibles may give you current pleasure, but you should think about your collection as an expense, not an investment. Trying to accurately guess what will be valuable in the year 2020 is a lot harder than finding a couple of mutual funds that will double or triple in value by then.

Still bound and determined to have a collection of something? Why not try stocks and bonds? They are a lot like collectibles: You add to them regularly and you can keep them for years.

Get an Early Start on Your Twenty-First-Century Life

The earlier you start, the easier it will be. That's because any mistakes you make—and be prepared for a few—can be rectified over time. An unwise investment or two won't derail your entire plan.

There's another advantage to starting early: It gives you more options for planning your retirement. If you start saving at age 45, there are fewer types of investments appropriate for building a retirement nest egg than if you start at age 30 when you can invest in a wider variety of things, some of which entail bigger risks but much bigger possible investment returns.

U.S. SAVINGS BONDS: NOT AS DORKY AS YOU THINK

Buying U.S. savings bonds is an easy way to start a stash of savings for retirement. A Series EE U.S. savings bond costs as little as $25. Buy one of these each week for a year and you'll have $1,300 at the end of the year. You can get Uncle Sam's bonds at most banks.

The bonds will earn interest, but the government has a complicated formula for determining that interest. For more information on savings bonds, write to Savings Bonds, Washington, DC 20026. For current interest rates on savings bonds, call (800) 872-6637.

Your youth does have some rewards when it comes to retirement planning. One big one is that you can make mistakes and take risks with your retirement investments. Do that when you are young and you'll reap the benefits when you are older.

Zero Is Zero, a Little Is More

Whatever you do now is a plus. Zero is zero now and it still is zero later. But even a little money invested now can translate into a lot more when you retrieve it from your investment account in 30 years.

It's not as hard as you think. If you're 25 years old now, start saving $2,000 a year for the next ten years. If you invest that money at 4 percent, by the time you're 65 years old, you will have $250,000. The zeros following that, or any other number, are a lot more than an account that reads all zeros.

In the next chapter, you'll discover how you can make your savings add zeros so you can get your retirement screenplay onto the silver screen when the silver graces your hair.

TAKING *care* of *numero* UNO

The flight attendants are right. Take care of yourself first and put the oxygen mask over your own face before the baby's. So it goes with your retirement plan. Your savings represent the **oxygen mask** you will need to survive. Pay yourself first, so you can take care of yourself and those you love when it comes **time to retire.**

Hundreds of times each day, thousands of times each year, airline flight attendants dispense a little piece of advice which represents the basic tenet of retirement planning.

Next time you are seated on the plane waiting for take-off, listen to the sound bite about oxygen masks: Take care of yourself first—always put the oxygen mask over

$1,000 THE EASY WAY

Want to save $1,000 a year? All you need to do is save $20 a week for 50 weeks (you get two weeks off for responsible behavior).

Eliminate these expenses and watch your retirement savings grow. And remember: Out-of-home food and beverages are huge budget busters. Cut back on these items so you will be able to indulge yourself with feasts galore all through your retirement.

• One coffeehouse **coffee** at $1.50-a-cup for five days = $7.50.

• One giant **muffin** or cookie = $1.50.

• One **beer** or glass of wine with tip and tax = $6.00.

• One **fast food** meal with tax = $5.00.

your own face before the baby's. You can't help anyone else if you are unconscious in your seat.

So it goes for your retirement plan. Consider your savings the oxygen mask you will need to survive. Pay yourself first, so you can take care of yourself and those you love when it comes time to retire. Nobody else is going to take care of you when you retire, and you certainly can't take care of anyone else if you don't have enough money saved.

Seven Savings Strategies (SSS)

You can put together a very comfortable sum for your retirement even if you are not earning $75,000 or $100,000 a year. Follow these seven savings strategies:

1. Make it easy on yourself. Get your employer to directly deposit retirement savings into your own or a company-sponsored account.

2. Save regularly. Get your employer to deduct money from every paycheck. Do it yourself if you don't have a company plan.

3. Save at least 10 percent of every paycheck and at least 30 percent from every bonus, dollar gift, or financial windfall that may come your way.

Numbers Galore

Use this formula to discover how compounding will make your money grow:

$$I * (1 + R)^T = M$$

I = Your original investment
R = The interest rate, or rate of return, on your investment
T = The time your investment gathers interest
M = The money you will have amassed

Thus, the formula for determining the value of a $2,000 original investment at 8 percent over five years is:

$2,000 \times (1 + .08)^5$ or 2,000 x (1.08 x 1.08 x 1.08 x 1.08 x 1.08)

After five years, your $2,000 investment will be worth $2,938.

You're Getting Older Every Day

Waiting ten years to start your retirement savings plan can be costly. Look at the difference between what a 30-year-old and a 40-year-old must save each year to maintain a similar comfortable retirement.

Current Income Level	Age 30	Age 40
$35,000	$ 4,035	$ 6,520
50,000	6,602	10,644
75,000	11,511	18,425

4. Start sooner rather than later. Early savings will earn you more retirement dollars than later savings.

5. Take advantage of tax loopholes for the money you put into a retirement plan.

6. Take advantage of tax loopholes on the money your investments earn.

7. Use other people's money. Let your employer contribute to your retirement savings.

SPLURGE, DON'T PLUNGE

It's okay to take some of that financial windfall you received from your great-grandmother and splurge a little. Go ahead and indulge in a vacation to the islands, a new computer system, or good quality living room furniture.

Just make sure that your purchase doesn't cost you a bundle in the future. That $35,000 sports car will not only raise your insurance rates year after year, but the constant repair-shop costs can be a long-term drain on your finances.

SSS 1: Earn $680 in 30 Minutes

Make saving easy for yourself by enlisting your boss in the endeavor. Have your employer directly deposit retirement savings into a company-sponsored account such as a 401(k) plan. You can't spend money you never get your hands on.

If your employer doesn't offer such an account, contact your employee benefits department. Ask to have at least 10 percent deposited into the IRA account you have established on your own. You may need to get some forms from the custodian of your IRA and then turn them over to your employer.

Your payback for taking the 30 minutes to do this? Invest $2,000 a year in a tax-deductible account, and you save yourself $560 in taxes in the 28 percent tax bracket. Now factor in the 6 percent let's say you earn on the $2,000 invested and you get another $120. That's $680 for 30 minutes of work in the first year alone.

SSS 2: Don a Habit

You can save consistently even without the help of an employer. Some companies won't directly deposit a portion of your earnings into a retirement plan. And if you're a consultant or freelancer, you don't have access to that kind of infrastructure that makes deposits in a savings or retirement plan on a regular basis. This just means you need a little more discipline to get into the habit yourself.

You can get your bank to deposit money directly into your account or you can do it the old-fashioned way: you cash your paycheck at the bank, count the dollars, and immediately put at least 10 percent into the retirement account you have established on your own.

SSS 3: Here a Percentage, There a Percentage

Save at least 10 percent of every paycheck. Once you've done that, you will find it's easier to save money you didn't expect to get. That means saving at least 30 percent from every bonus you receive or every check your parents send you for your birthday or holiday.

A word on inherited money. Put at least 30 percent into your retirement treasure chest. Use the remaining funds to pay any debts you have. That means wiping your credit card balances clean. If you still have some money, make an extra payment on your mortgage or pay one extra month of rent.

$1,000 THE EASY WAY: THE SEQUEL

Want to save another $1,000 a year? Try this:

• Instead of renting a **movie** for $3.00 or more, look for a good one on TV.

• Instead of eating out in even a very inexpensive restaurant, save the $10.00 and treat yourself to an **ice cream** cone after dinner at an ice cream parlor.

• Bring your own **popcorn** to the movies and save the $3.00 they charge.

• Take a **walk** instead of the $1.50 bus ride.

Reform your spending habits now for a healthy retirement later.

SSS 4: Compounding: Time Really Is Money

Einstein really was on to something with that $E = MC^2$ equation, which stated that energy can be converted to mass and mass to energy, and that somehow the rate of speed at which you travel makes time go faster or slower.

There's a corollary to that in the investment universe. The concept is called compounding. It says that not only does invested money grow over time, but your old invested dollars earn more than your new invested dollars.

Here's how that magic works: Invest $1,000 in year one at 10 percent, and at the end of the year you have $1,000 plus 10 percent of $1,000 or $100, for a total of $1,100. In year two, you let that $1,100 earn another 10 percent and you invest another $1,000. In year two, your original $1,000 earns more than your second $1,000 does.

FACTOID

Life expectancy has increased by almost 30 years during the twentieth century. Some experts predict that by the year 2020, women will have a life expectancy of 80 years, while men will lag about 6 1/2 years behind.

That means your retirement will probably be longer than is typical now. So you'll need to save enough money for the extra years you'll hopefully have.

Year One $1,000 in Year Two:
$1,000 + (10% of $1,000 or $100) = $1,100

Year Two $1,000 in Year Two:
$1,000 + (10% of $1,100 or $110) = $1,210

Compound Magic

Like that battery bunny who keeps going and going and going, compounding makes your investments keep growing and growing and growing. Over the years, compounding can turn a very modest investment into a very comfortable retirement sum.

Thanks to compounding, if you double the interest—or rate of return—you get on your investment, you can more than double the amount of money you amass. Take a look at what compounding can do for just one $1,000 investment.

Social Security: How Much Will You Receive?

Ever wonder how much Social Security will pay you when you retire? Getting the information is surprisingly easy, and it's a freebie government service.

1. Call the Social Security Administration at (800) 772-1213 and ask for a form called "Request for Earnings and Benefit Estimate Statement." You will receive the form in a week or two.

2. Complete the form. You may find question number nine troublesome. It asks you to estimate your average annual earnings between now and when you retire. Just take the total of your earnings last year and multiply it by the number of years until you think you may want to retire. Send in the form. You'll get a statement in about a month.

3. Read the statement. Your estimated monthly Social Security income probably will be rather low. Don't despair. It's a good bet you will be making more money in the future, even after discounting for inflation, than you are now. Your Social Security income will reflect that. Think of your estimated Social Security income as the absolute rock-bottom amount you can expect to get from the government.

Years	4%	6%	8%	10%	12%
1	$1,040	$1,060	$1,080	$1,100	$1,120
2	1,080	1,130	1,170	1,210	1,250
3	1,120	1,190	1,260	1,330	1,400
4	1,170	1,260	1,360	1,460	1,570
5	1,220	1,340	1,470	1,610	1,760
10	1,480	1,790	2,160	2,590	3,110
15	1,180	2,400	3,170	4,180	5,470
20	2,190	3,210	4,660	6,730	9,640
25	2,280	2,400	5,030	7,400	10,800

SSS 5 and 6: Give Yourself a Break

When you save for your retirement, Uncle Sam rewards you with tax breaks. The money you put into a tax-deferred retirement account—at work or in an IRA you establish yourself—actually reduces the amount of taxes you pay. Take a look at what this means if your annual income is $40,000 with and without a $2,000 retirement contribution in a tax-qualified plan.

	Without Contribution	With Contribution
Income	$40,000	$40,000
Retirement contribution	0	2,000
Taxable income	40,000	38,000
Taxes at 28%	11,200	10,640

That's a $560 difference which you get to pay yourself rather than Uncle Sam when you deposit your money into a tax-qualified plan.

It gets better. There's another tax break you get by investing in a qualified plan. Let's say your $2,000 earned 10 percent interest, or $200. You don't pay taxes on that earned money either until you withdraw it at retirement. Until then, your contributions grow tax-deferred. So you can add that $200 in interest to the $560 you saved in taxes and you've got $760 more.

SSS 7: Use Other People's Money

Taking advantage of a 401(k) plan is a smart move. It's positively brilliant if your employer matches some or a portion of your contribution to the fund.

A few, very generous firms match equal amounts of company money for every dollar you set aside. Your $2,000 contribution becomes $4,000 with your employer's money. A match of 25 percent to 50 percent is more common, but still a very good deal because you don't have to pay taxes on that money until you withdraw it from the account.

Spending in Wonderland

Remember when Alice ate a cookie in Wonderland that made her shrink and then ate another that turned her into giant proportions? Think of spending as the incredible-shrinking-retirement-plan cookie and saving as the giant-retirement-plan cookie.

Believe it or not, it costs more to spend than to save. Saved money buys you more than spent money. The penalty for spending is even greater when you add in taxes. Conversely, the reward you get for putting your money into a tax-deductible account like an IRA or a 401(k) plan is even greater.

Here's how it works: Let's say you earn $40,000. After the rent or mortgage, your utilities, your groceries, and clothing, you've got $5,000 to spend or save.

CONQUERING THE BIG D THAT STANDS FOR DEBT

Pay cash. Debt experts find that people who pay cash typically spend 25 percent to 30 percent less than credit card users. Cash users also avoid interest and late charges.

Consolidate loans…maybe. This works only if the consolidated loan carries a lower interest rate than the debt you are paying off and if you use all the extra money you save by consolidating to pay off your debts. Don't spend the funds on a vacation.

The spend-it-all plan:

Money available	$5,000
You spend it all	5,000
You have	0
Taxes (28% of $5,000)	1,400
(Now you've got to borrow that $1,400 to pay Uncle Sam.)	

Now pay Uncle Sam first and then spend what's left over.

Money available	$5,000
Taxes (28% of $5000)	1,400
You spend the rest	3,600
Money spent but not invested	3,600

Now look what happens when you put just $2,000 of that $5,000 into a pretax account.

Money available	$5,000
Money into tax-deductible plan	2,000
Money on which you pay taxes	3,000
Taxes (28% of $3000)	840
Money left over to spend	2,160

Under this plan, you will have $2,160 to spend on whatever you want and still have invested $2,000 for your future.

Get a Grip on Spending

The ability to save is directly related to how wisely you spend. Foolish purchases can account for 20 to 30 percent of your total spending. Here are some ways to make sure you don't waste the money you work so hard to earn.

• Stop using credit cards.

• Stick your loose change into a piggy bank.

- Shop with a list and stick to it. Avoid impulse buys.

- Look for bargains, sales, and outlet stores. Comparison shop and use coupons.

- Quit smoking. You'll save money on cigarettes, car and life insurance, and medical bills.

- Buy generic.

- Haunt garage sales and second-hand shops.

- Buy a less expensive economy car.

- Take the bus or subway. Better yet, walk (it's healthier, too).

- Eat dinner at home, brown-bag it at work.

- Refinance high-rate loans.

- Rent items you don't often use.

- Swap services, time, and tools with friends and neighbors.

- Maintain what you own and do your own repair work.

- Go to the library instead of buying books.

CONQUERING THE BIG D THAT STANDS FOR DEBT

Here are some tips for paying down high credit card balances.

• Use credit cards only in **emergency** situations, such as getting your car towed.

• Pay your bill **on time** to avoid late charges.

• Start paying at least two to three times **more** than the monthly minimum.

Not All Debt Is Created Equal

Debt comes in all shapes and sizes. Traditional debt is for a specific amount of money, at a fixed or floating interest rate, and for a specific amount of time. The higher the interest rate, the longer it will take you to pay off the debt or the bigger the monthly payment you'll have. The longer the period of the loan, the lower your monthly payment but the greater the total amount of money you will pay for that loan.

Credit card debt combines the worst features of a traditional loan. The interest rate is high, and the time frame for repayment is infinite. The minimum fee often covers only the interest. Thus, if you pay only the rock-bottom fee each month, you may still be paying for items bought in your twenties when you get ready to retire in your sixties.

Worse yet, it's a good bet that the items you put on plastic are worth considerably less today than when you bought them.

Of course, into your life a little debt will always fall. But keep it to a minimum to avoid being flooded. Cutting your debt is one of the best avenues to financial security you can take.

RETIREMENT MYTH AND REALITY

Myth: With your house paid off by the time you retire, your expenses will be modest.

Reality: Your property taxes, utilities, and general maintenance most likely will continue to increase.

Debt as an Investment

Taking on some debt can be a wise decision when the thing you are financing increases in value. A loan to finance education or to bolster your skills in the workplace can be a good move if that allows you to earn more money over the years. The money you spend on a home mortgage gives you a place to live, some tax deductions, and an investment that you can sell.

You may need to get a loan for that twentieth-century necessity—the automobile. But unlike education or a home, the value of your car decreases over time, while your loan payments remain fixed. Investigate the reliability and average annual maintenance of any auto you buy.

Escape from the Plastic Prison

To bring that MasterCard balance down to zero, you are going to have to start paying a lot more each month. There's no way around that. Where will you get the funds? From the money you save by going to half-priced movies and forgoing mocha cappuccinos.

Why not put that money into an investment account for a year and then use that money to pay off the credit card? Because most investments will not earn as much money as the interest you are being charged on your credit card.

Compare what a $1,000 credit card balance will cost you over a year with what a reasonable rate of return of 8 percent will earn you on your savings.

> **$1,000 credit card balance at 15% = $1,150**
> **$1,000 investment plus return at 8% = $1,080**
> **Amount you still owe on your card (7% of $1000) = $70**

Saving to Stardom

You are not afraid to work hard, now don't be slack about saving just as hard. Keep in mind the tremendous rewards. Weigh those rewards against the heavy burden you carry when you spend and, worse still, put yourself in debt.

Remember, time is money. A regular savings plan started now will get you a bundle of money when you retire. Start early and you can be a regular couch potato as you watch your investments grow to grandiose proportions.

Cheap Thrills

- Nature **hikes and bird watching.** Most national parks, as well as many state and local parks, offer wildlife tours with experienced guides.

- Festivals and **fairs.**

- **Museum** field trips.

- City **walking** tours.

- **Cemetery tours.** They can enlighten you about local history as well as be fascinating.

- **Factory and farm tours.** Wineries, chocolate factories, and other businesses offer free or low-cost tours and also provide freebies to sample.

- Poetry and **book** readings.

- **Birthplaces** of historical figures, such as presidents, authors, and other local luminaries.

- Public **library** programs and film festivals.

- Programs and **lectures** at colleges and universities.

- **Sports** programs offered by adult education programs at local schools.

- **Night court.** Just like on TV, an interesting parade of citizenry shows up at the local courthouse to battle an array of offenses. Members of the public can sit in the gallery and watch for free.

CLIMB
to the top
of the
investment
TOWER

Putting together a retirement plan is a lot like feeding yourself. When you feel hungry for some macaroni and cheese, you take your money to the grocery store. You either buy the premade stuff or purchase the individual items of macaroni, cheese, and milk. At home, you heat the prepared casserole or assemble the individual items and then cook them.

That feeding endeavor had three components:

- Money for the food

- Shopping for the food

- Preparing the food

Assembling a retirement plan consists of three similar components:

- Money for investments

- Shopping for investments

- Setting up investment accounts

The Investment Grocery Store

Now that you know how to save the dollars you need for retirement, you can tackle the task of putting your money into some investments to make it grow. Shopping for investments is like going to the grocery store. There are thousands of different types of investment items. They come in different sizes and they are packaged in a myriad of ways. Some are better bargains than others, and you can buy the items at thousands of different outlets.

The one big difference between these shopping experiences is that unlike grocery shopping, there are thousands of people and institutions who are willing—for a fee— to help you buy investments. Many of these helpers—stockbrokers, bankers, insurance salespeople, for instance—also run their own investment grocery stores. They make their money by steering you into their stores even though you may be able to buy the same investment items elsewhere for a lot less money.

The investment supermarket may seem totally baffling at first. While you already may recognize some of the labeled items such as stocks, bonds, and mutual funds, it can get a little confusing when you encounter other generically labeled items such as high-yield mutual bond funds, variable-rate annuities, or growth-and-income mutual funds. Your choices further multiply when you realize that the brokerage firm Merrill Lynch, the bank Wells Fargo, and the insurance company Metropolitan Life all offer brand-name items, as well.

The Four Generic Investments

With so many offerings, how do you choose the investment items that are best for you? Let's simplify the items into categories. Generic groceries fall into three basic categories:

- Fresh food that needs to be refrigerated

- Frozen food that goes into a freezer

- Everything else that goes on your pantry shelves

Similarly, there are four generic types of investments:

- *Equity investments* such as stocks and stock mutual funds and real estate. When you invest in equities, you are buying a portion of a company or a property. You become an owner or shareholder. The people who run the company may also give you a share of the profits in the form of a divi-dend, which usually is paid four times a year. Scores of different factors can and do change the value of your equity share.

- *Debt investments* such as bonds. When you invest in a bond or other debt instrument, you actually are loaning your money with the promise that it will be paid back on a specific date. The time period of the loan is called the maturity. You also get a regular payment at a specific rate—the inter-est rate—on the money you lend.

- *Combination debt and equity instruments* such as convertible stocks and bonds. A convertible bond is a bond—or debt instrument—that you can convert into an equity instrument such as a stock.

- *Cash and cash-equivalents* such as certificates of deposit and money market funds. Most cash-equivalents are debt instruments with very, very short-term maturities—six months or less are standard. The value fluctuates very little, and often there is no fee for buying and selling these investments. They usually earn a low interest rate, but they tend to be very safe investments. Although they are great places to put money you may need quickly, because the interest rates are so low they are terrible places to put a lot of long-term investments such as your retirement money.

Packaged Investments

You can buy individual investment items such as IBM stock or an AT&T bond. You can also buy a package consisting of a number of different individual items. The most common packaged investments are called mutual funds, or just plain funds, and there are over 7,500 from which to choose.

Don't panic over all the choices. Just remember that these mutual funds invest in (1) equities, (2) debt, (3) debt and equities, or cash. Each of these categories can be further subdivided.

The big advantage of investing in a mutual fund rather than investing in individual stocks and bonds is that you get to put a little bit of money into a lot of different investments. That also lets you spread your risk around: That's called diversification, a basic tenet of investing. The low value of one poorly performing company in the fund can be offset by a large rise in value of another.

Investments Have Personalities

Your basic personality traits are big factors in determining and shaping how you act and react to the world around you. While your personality is composed of hundreds of different traits, a psychological evaluation might focus on just a few pairs of those traits. Are you introverted or extroverted, persuasive or assertive, analytical or amiable, judgmental or perceptive? Since no one is totally introverted without some extroverted qualities, evaluating each pair of traits involves a sliding scale.

Like people, investments have defining characteristics which can be evaluated on a sliding scale. Fortunately for your sanity, there are only a few important investment traits to keep in mind.

High Risk versus Low Risk

Some investments are riskier than others. Obviously, everyone would like to invest in something that is totally risk-free, but that is not possible.

Even cash as an investment has risk. It actually carries a bigger risk than stocks because cash runs the very high risk—almost a total certainty—of being diminished by inflation. That means the same face value will be worth much less in 30 years than it is today. Stocks and mutual funds, though, have appreciated faster than inflation has been able to eat away at those values.

There are all kinds of risks. Some risks have a bigger effect on one type of investment than another; but each and every investment carries some risk. Moderately high-risk investments can be excellent items to fuel-inject your retirement plan because they usually have higher rates of return. In the investing world, being too conservative and too risk-averse can be as big a mistake as being too aggressive or risk-seeking.

High Rate of Return versus Low Rate of Return

The rate of return of an investment is usually related to how risky the investment is. In theory, the bigger the risk you take, the bigger the reward you will get in the form of a rate of return.

The most perfect investment would have a high rate of return but be extremely safe. Don't waste your time searching for that investment. It doesn't exist.

Not so for the investment with a low rate of return and high risk. A frightening example might be bonds in a bankrupt company (high risk) which carry an interest rate of 3 percent (low rate of return). Usually, the rate of return is less than it might be because someone—the sales company or salesperson—is getting paid high fees.

Steer clear of such losers. If you are going to take the risk, you deserve at least a good chance of getting a high rate of return.

THE THREE FACES OF RETIREMENT INCOME

Expect your total retirement income to come from three sources:

• 1/3 from Social Security

• 1/3 from your employer-sponsored plans

• 1/3 from your personal savings

If your estimated Social Security income is significantly less than 1/3 of your current income, you are going to have to make up the difference elsewhere. Take command of your future with a retirement plan that you control. Save and invest as much as you can today, so you can enjoy your twenty-first-century retirement years.

Liquid versus Illiquid

Liquidity is a term which describes how quickly and easily you are able to sell an investment for cash. Your home is a very illiquid investment because it may take you months to find a buyer willing to meet your price. A certificate of deposit is a pretty liquid investment because you usually can get cash for it immediately. Be careful though, because you will be subject to a penalty if you withdraw your money earlier than you agreed to.

Most investments lie in the middle. You don't have to worry a lot about the liquidity of an investment you make for your retirement because you don't need to sell those investments for cash for another 20 to 40 years.

Short-Term versus Long-Term

While your retirement money will be invested for a long period of time, some investments are designed to rise in value over a longer period of time than others. Your home is a long-term investment. You buy your house and keep it for a number of years, or even decades. A certificate of deposit represents a short-term investment because it stops paying interest after a year or two.

Combining the Investment Traits

Certain investment traits tend to be paired with other investment traits, just as certain personality traits seem to go together.

Here are a few investment personality traits that tend to be found together. Exceptions exist, of course, but keep these trait pairings in mind when you are investing for your retirement.

- The greater the investment risk, the bigger the investment return.

- Long-term investments provide bigger rates of return than short-term investments.

- Short-term investments tend to be more liquid than long-term investments.

The Investment Tower

This tower—built from blocks of specific investments—lets you see how investments stack up according to risk and rate of return. The following are ranked from top to bottom: highest risk to lowest, and highest to lowest potential rate of return.

High risk	Futures contracts
	Collectibles
	Options
	Raw land
	Junk bonds/Foreign investments
Moderate risk	Mortgage-backed securities/Stock and bond mutual funds
	Corporate bonds
	Rental real estate

Low risk   Blue-chip stocks

Life insurance contracts

U.S. Treasury bonds

Short-term bond funds

Annuities

Zero coupon bonds

Utility stocks

Cash/Bank CDs/U.S. Treasury bills

Checking accounts/GICs
(guaranteed investment contracts)/Savings accounts

Money market funds and accounts

Money Market Funds versus Money Market Accounts

They may sound like the same investment animal, but there are some big differences between a money market account and a money market fund. Simply put, a money market account is a place to put money, while a money market fund is a type of investment.

Money market accounts are offered by banks, savings and loan institutions, and credit unions. They act like checking accounts that pay interest but let you write only a limited number of checks. The money in your account—up to $100,000—is insured by the government. The interest rate you get on your money is low and it varies, but you can withdraw your money immediately and without paying any penalty.

Money market funds are not insured, but they can act like limited checking accounts. These funds usually pay a higher interest rate than money market accounts. The money you place in these funds is invested in short-term securities. Some funds invest only in government securities; others in certificates of deposit and in government and corporate securities; and still others only in nontaxable state and U.S. government securities.

Every dollar you put into a money market fund gets you one share. You can let the interest earned on your share go back into your account to buy more shares, or you can withdraw the interest when you earn it.

Money market accounts and funds can be good places to put money you will need over the short term. They are terrible places for your retirement savings because these accounts and funds earn low interest rates.

Where to Put Your Money in the Tower

Look to put the bulk of your money into investments toward the top, but not at the top, of the tower where you get a higher rate of return. The higher the rate, the more money you'll have when you retire.

Avoid the very top of the tower, where investments are highly speculative. Futures contracts are not only very risky, but they cost tens of thousands of dollars for just one contract. The worst thing about them is you can lose more money than you invested in the first place.

You can buy a contract worth $100,000 for just $5,000. Sounds good, but if the value of that $100,000 contract falls to $80,000 at the end of the day, you must fork over your $5,000 contract plus another $15,000 in cash at the end of that day to cover the $20,000 price decline.

The View from Almost the Top of the Tower

Three-quarters of the way up the tower is the investment spot for your retirement savings to grow at a good rate of return. If you stay too low on the tower, your investments will grow a lot more slowly and you'll have to invest more money at the lower levels than at the higher levels to amass a similar amount of money over the years.

Invest $1,000 for 25 years at 4 percent and you'll have only $2,280. Double your rate of return to 8 percent and your money more than doubles to $5,030. Go for a 12 percent return and you've got $10,800, or more than ten times your original investment, after 25 years.

Your Investment Friends

To make your savings work as hard as possible, your retirement investments should be concentrated among stock and bond mutual funds, mortgage-backed securities, and corporate bonds. You'll be spending most of your money on these investment friends in that area of the tower, so get to know them a little better. Here are some personality profiles of stock funds you might consider:

- *Income funds* invest in the equity shares of older, well-established companies. These businesses—often gas and electric companies—tend to grow slowly but steadily, and they pay relatively large dividends compared to their stock price. You can reinvest these dividends into more equity shares or have them paid to you directly, in which case you get income from the fund.

- *Growth funds* invest in young companies that need a lot of money but may grow very fast. They usually pay low or no dividends. The value of these shares can rise substantially and very quickly or plunge steeply and swiftly.

- *Growth and income funds* invest in both growth and income companies. Income typically is less than in growth funds, but the value of the shares has the potential for bigger price increases than in income funds.

- *Aggressive growth funds* invest in companies that are newer and more on the cutting edge than growth companies. The rate of failure for these companies is high. Those that succeed offer the potential for spectacular price increases.

- *Mortgage-backed securities* are actually government bonds that carry a higher risk and usually a higher rate of return than a standard U.S. Treasury bond. Your investment is backed by mortgages—issued to people just like you— that the governnment has insured.

The World of Bonds

Sometimes the simplest things are the hardest to understand. Bonds and bond funds totally baffle most people because bonds behave very differently from stocks.

When you buy the stock of a company, you are buying a portion—sometimes called a share—of that company. The value of your ownership stake—the price of the stock—rises and falls, to a large degree, according to the success that company has in selling its products and services and making a profit.

A bond is the flip side of a stock or equity share. A bond, essentially, is a loan. When you buy a bond from the government or from a corporation or a share in a bond fund, you become a lender. The loan you make is for a specific time period, called the maturity of the loan. The borrower promises to pay you, at the time of maturity, all the money you lent it.

At the time you make the loan, the borrower—whether it's the government or a corporation—also agrees to pay you regular fees (or interest) on the loan. That fee is a specific, fixed amount, which is why bonds are known as fixed-income investments.

Let's say you buy a $10,000 bond from Computer Keyboard Corporation (CKC). You have lent CKC $10,000. CKC agrees to pay back the $10,000 at the end of ten years and it also agrees to pay you 6 percent interest—or $600—each year for the use of your money. Thus, you have a fixed income of $600 every year from the bond.

Split-Personality Bonds

The tricky part about understanding bonds comes when you want to sell the bond—or just determine the value of a bond—before it matures. Here is where interest rates come into play and the investment trait that gives bonds a split personality. While a rise in interest rates boosts the rate a bond pays (that is the coupon rate), that rise in interest rates will depress the actual price of the bond.

Imagine that interest rates have fallen since you bought your bond and that CKC is now willing to pay only 4 percent each year—or $400—to borrow money from people like you. Obviously, the value of your bond will rise because your bond pays $600 each year, which is better than the new CKC bond which pays only $400 annually.

Time passes and interest rates rise. Now CKC can borrow money at 8 percent or $800 a year, but you still hold your CKC bond which pays only $600 every 12 months. What happens to the value of your bond? It falls, because other investors would rather hold a CKC bond paying $800 a year than one paying $600.

That's why bond prices move in the opposite direction from interest rates. Just remember, when interest rates fall, bond prices rise, and when interest rates rise, bond prices fall.

Taking Stock of Interest Rates

As with bonds, interest rate movements also affect equity prices, but in a less direct and severe way. Generally, rising interest rates and inflation put a damper on stock prices while declining rates boost equity prices.

But, there are numerous exceptions to this rule-of-thumb. A lot depends on what's happening in the fixed-income markets.

Extremely high interest rates can make short-term, fixed-rate investments such as CDs more popular than stocks. Investors then sell their stocks and buy CDs, which depresses the stock prices.

Long-term investors, though, watch the market gyrations from the stadium skybox high above the short-term bond and stock price fracas on the field. They invest through bull and bear markets, secure in the knowledge that a steady and consistent savings and investment strategy will create a winning portfolio for their retirement years.

Don't Forget Social Security

The Social Security deductions from your paycheck also represent investments for your retirement. You don't have any choice in how much the government deducts or how that money is invested. But the government promises that you will have the option to receive a specific amount of money every month come retirement.

You will have the option to begin receiving those payments between ages 62 and 67.

If you opt to start getting benefits at age 62, you receive a smaller monthly check than if you wait until you are 67 years old.

You're Almost There

Your retirement plan needs a few more items, in addition to your investments, to be complete: real estate, insurance, and your treasure trove of friends, interests, and experiences.

- *Real estate:* Buy a home and you've got that piece in your long-term plan. You can also buy real estate by purchasing shares in a mutual fund that specializes in buying property.

- *Insurance:* You'll need different types of insurance to protect different types of assets. Life insurance protects your family in the event that you die and are no longer earning money to help pay the bills. Health insurance protects you from giant medical bills that could total more than all your assets. Home insurance protects you from paying the full cost of replacing a roof when the hurricane knocks a tree through it. Chapter eight will help you understand the different types of insurance, what insurance covers, and how much you really need.

- *Your treasure trove:* Friends and family and the relationships you build with them will provide the most satisfying aspect of your retirement. You'll also want to nurture your own personality traits and talents which comfort you in times of stress and allow you to fully relish the times of joy. And do remember to exercise your intellect as much as you exercise your body.

CONQUERING THE BIG D THAT STANDS FOR DEBT

Pay off **unnecessary debts.** Here you can use two tactics: You can pay down the debt with the highest interest rate. That saves the most money. You also might entirely pay off one small debt. That will give you a very rewarding feeling of accomplishment.

The Plan's Complete

Your retirement plan now looks like this:

- Investments

- Real estate

- Insurance

- Treasure trove

Next we'll take a look at where to shop for investments and places to put them.

UNCLE Sam and your retirement PLANS

CHAPTER FIVE

You've got your knapsack of savings and you've got the clues you need to invest those savings. Your next step is to get your investments into a place like an **IRA** *account or a* **401(k)** *plan where Uncle Sam can't touch them. Yes, there are such* **oases.**

You've got some very appealing opportunities to thumb your nose at Mr. Taxman. Your choices are not so many as to make your decision difficult, but enough to put you at the control panel of your retirement pleasure machine so you can leave the IRS standing by the road in the dust.

To decide which accounts are best for you, you need to focus on the advantages a plan offers you NOW. Don't worry about the complicated schedules for withdrawing your investments from your retirement accounts later. You've got plenty of time between now and when you retire to do that.

Greed Is Good

If you already have some type of retirement account going, you might be tempted to skip this chapter. Don't do that. Learning about other types of accounts will not be a waste of your time. When it comes to establishing a retirement account, greed is good. Go for more than just one. Here's why.

It's a good bet that you'll probably work for more than one employer in your lifetime. As you move from job to job, the retirement plan offered by each organization will change. Understanding your options gives you greater control over your future. And any account you put in place now will not close out future options. It just gives you more flexibility.

Even if you're someone who works for one employer your entire lifetime, it's smart to set up your own retirement account. There are advantages to having more than one retirement duffel bag.

Eat Dust, Mr. Taxman

The difference between a tax-advantaged retirement account and a regular investment account with a stockbroker like Merrill Lynch or a mutual fund company like Fidelity is whether or not you have to pay taxes on the money that's in there until you withdraw it.

Some tax-advantaged plans allow you to deduct the contributions you make from your taxable income. This lowers the amount of taxes you pay in the tax year in which you make your contribution. The more you contribute, the lower your taxes will be.

All tax-advantaged plans give you a tax holiday on the money you earn on your investments. You don't have to pay taxes on those investment returns until you start withdrawing the funds. Sheltering from the IRS an 8 percent return on your investments may not seem very significant, but it is, thanks to that magic act of compounding. Invest $2,000 a year at 8 percent for 30 years and your compounded tax-deferred earnings amount to $28,334.

Take the Joyride, Dude

Disable the IRS's tax-chase car and take as many joyrides as possible on your employer's wheels. That's the two-part strategy for your retirement account.

While the IRS dodge is obvious, the freebies your employer offers may be less visible. They're worth uncovering so you can take advantage of them.

You wouldn't say no to an all-expense paid trip to a luxury resort in an exotic locale or free movie passes to any theater anywhere for a lifetime or even gratis groceries for a week. So make sure you don't pass on the retirement plan offerings that are yours for the taking from your employer. The value of taking part in these plans—whether they're straight pensions, profit sharing, or 401(k)s—is worth a lot more than free flicks.

Not only are the plans themselves good deals, but employers often will kick their money into your plan. That's free money to you—think of it as a salary raise. Best of all, you don't pay any taxes on the money your boss puts into your account until you start withdrawing your investments.

Something for Everyone

The plans or accounts you choose largely depend on your employment situation. No matter what that may be, there's at least one plan for you. IRAs are available to everyone. You can often participate in pension and 401(k) plans if you are a staff employee. For the self-employed, there are Keogh plans in a couple of different shapes.

COMMON IRA AND 401(K) MISTAKES

The government gives you the opportunity to be really dumb with your **tax-deferred** IRA and 401(k) plan investments. Don't put your money in low-rate-of-return money market funds or other low-yielding investments like CDs. Why shelter $2,000 that has only a **2.5 percent** rate of return? Invest in high-return vehicles. Let the low-rate investments sit in non–tax-deferred accounts. Of course, anything with a higher rate of return does carry more **risk.** But if you're starting your investment plans early enough, you have plenty of time to recoup any losses you may incur.

What's the Point of an IRA If I Can't Deduct It?

The point is the money you make on your investments does not get taxed in an IRA until you withdraw the money at retirement.

Compare how your investments grow faster and get bigger in a non-deductible IRA than they do in a regular account in which you pay taxes on the money your investments earn. Assume you are in the 28 percent tax bracket and invest $2,000 each year in a nondeductible IRA.

Years to Retirement	IRA Account at 8%	Regular Account at 8%
10	$ 26,461	$ 26,066
15	47,499	45,710
20	77,097	71,707
25	119,273	106,091
30	179,928	151,594

IRA advantage to you: $179,928 – $151,594 = $28,334

Your IRA Utility Vehicle

The utility vehicle of retirement plans is the IRA—the Individual Retirement Account. It's reliable, easy to drive, and goes everywhere. It can also haul just about any investment you care to stick in it.

Created by the U.S. government in 1974, the IRA originally was designed for people who did not have an employer-sponsored pension plan. The idea underlying the IRA—and almost every retirement plan out there—is that you save money during your younger years when your income and salary is high, let the money grow free from taxes, and then withdraw the funds when you are set to retire and your income is lower. At that time, you pay taxes on your retirement funds as you withdraw them.

If your income during your retirement years is lower, so is your tax rate. Thus, you end up paying lower taxes when you withdraw the funds than you would have paid on those investments when you were working. In short, the government shifts society's total tax burden from the older folks onto the younger folks. In effect, the big bite Uncle Sam is taking from your paycheck now is, in part, being used to fund your parents' IRAs.

The IRA Rules

You can deposit as much as $2,000—$4,000 if you're married—into an IRA every year and the money from those investments grows tax-deferred. As an individual, you can deduct $2,000 of that

CALL IT SIMPLE

As of January 1, 1997, there's a new SIMPLE plan for small businesses.

Uncle Sam recently made available a retirement plan for small employers who want to offer some type of retirement plan for their workers. Employers with 100 or fewer employees can now establish a Savings Incentive Match Plan for Employees (SIMPLE) retirement plan.

Under a SIMPLE plan, you can contribute up to $6,000 a year, before taxes, to an account that acts like an IRA or 401(k) plan.

If your employer doesn't offer a SIMPLE plan, it may be because the boss doesn't know about them yet. A gentle suggestion could earn you bonus points from your boss, kudos from your coworkers, and a comfortable retirement for you.

investment from your taxes. You and your spouse can deduct $4,000 even if your spouse is not working.

If either you or your spouse is covered by a pension plan, however, you can't deduct your contributions. Your W-2 form will tell you if you are covered by such a plan. Look for the little box labeled "pension plan." If it's checked, you're covered. If it's blank, you're not and you can deduct away.

What happens if you are covered by a pension plan, but you have chosen not to participate or have not been vested—eligible, right now, to receive future benefits—in the plan? Unfortunately, Uncle Sam still won't let you make the deduction.

How Do I Get an IRA?

While grocery stores have not yet gotten into the IRA business, you will find that just about any financial institution will gladly help you open an IRA. Banks, brokerage firms, mutual funds, and insurance companies are all competing for your money. You just fill out a little paperwork and fork over your money.

With so many people courting you, you can be selective about whom you choose. Comparison shop as you do for your clothes and groceries. Here's what you should consider when picking an institution.

- Are you being charged a fee? What is it for? Find out up front if the fees you are being charged are one-time service fees or ongoing fees for maintaining your account.

- What type of investments does the institution offer to you to put in your IRA? The more choices, the better for you. Look for a selection of bonds and bond funds as well as growth and growth-and-income funds.

- How have the investments offered performed over the years? Ask to see the rate of return for the investments. Look at the one-year, three-year, five-year, and ten-year numbers.

As Many IRAs as You Want

You can establish as many IRAs as you want in as many different places as you want. Each financial institution is going to charge you a fee, but you can avoid paying ten fees to ten different institutions by paying one fee to only one bank or brokerage firm. Involve fewer institutions and you'll also get fewer statements in the mail. The paperwork at tax time will be easier, too.

What Investments Go into an IRA?

Just about any standard investment can go into your IRA: stocks, bonds, mutual funds, Treasury bills and notes, certificates of deposit, and zero coupon bonds, to name a few.

What can't you stick into your IRA? That insurance policy the salesman told you was a "great investment" may be just that, but it can't go into your IRA. Other no-nos include: art, antiques, stamps, gold and silver coins minted outside the U.S., any physical real estate, and your collection of Disney celluloid.

Bored with Bonds and I Want to Switch

You can change the investments you have in your IRA. Let's say that you put your $2,000 of IRA money into a bond mutual fund. Five years pass. Now you want to switch your investment to a stock mutual fund. Just instruct the bank or brokerage firm holding your IRA to do that. You'll have to pay a commission fee for the transaction, but Uncle Sam imposes no penalty for the move. You can switch from investment to investment as many times as you want.

Bored with My Bank and I Want to Switch

You can also transfer any existing IRA account from one institution to another. Here, you have to be careful with the paperwork. Make sure the switch is a trustee-to-trustee transfer. In a trustee-to-trustee transfer, you never take possession of your IRA funds. Instead, you authorize the institution holding your IRA to transfer it to another institution. Fail to do that and you will pay a huge tax penalty. The penalty the government imposes on you is just horrendous for any other way of transferring your IRA. Mess up and you'll pay ordinary income taxes on all the money in the account plus another 10 percent tax penalty.

When Can I Get My IRA Money?

The magic age is 59 1/2. You can then start withdrawing the money. If you try to withdraw any earlier, you will incur a very severe (10 percent) tax penalty. There are a slew of exceptions to this rule, but the government will probably change the rules and the exceptions at least a couple of times before you get close to retirement.

Okay, there are not quite that many exceptions to the general rule. Still, there are a lot of complex specifications that do allow short-term or early withdrawals from your IRA account.

You can tap your account to pay for qualified medical and dental expenses that exceed 7.5 percent of your adjusted gross income. Of course, you will have to pay regular income tax on the amount you withdraw.

If you are unemployed and have received unemployment compensation for at least 12 consecutive weeks, you also can withdraw IRA funds without a tax penalty but only to help pay for medical insurance premiums—not out-of-pocket medical costs—for yourself and your family. Again, you must pay income tax on the money withdrawn.

You can withdraw an amount equal to or less than the premium price you pay. In this case, it doesn't make any difference whether you exceed the 7.5 percent adjusted gross income level.

You must make the IRA withdrawal, though, during the year in which you receive the unemployment compensation or in the following year, You can make the penalty-free IRA withdrawals for up to 60 days after you return to work.

You also can withdraw your IRA money if you are over 55 years old and retired. In this case you can withdraw a specified amount from your IRA over a specified number of years. You must adhere to the schedule, though, if you want to avoid tax penalties.

Tapping Your IRA for Medical Costs

The IRS does let you use your IRA money right now to pay some medical costs. You still must pay taxes on the money you withdraw, but you won't get hit with that other 10 percent penalty tax.

- If you are unemployed, you can use your IRA to pay your health insurance premiums.

- If your medical expenses—and those of your spouse and dependents—total more than 7.5 percent of your adjusted gross income, you can deduct money from your IRA to pay those expenses.

401(k) Plans: Like, Why Ask Why?

The only thing you've got a shot at that's better than a 401(k) plan is loving and being loved. End of discussion.

A 401(k) Short Story

- Some, but not all, employers offer 401(k) plans.

- Contributions you make to your 401(k) plan are pretax. Every year you can deduct up to $9,500, if you put that much in the plan.

- 401(k) plans are also known as defined-contribution plans because you define the contribution you make to the plan.

- Earnings on your investments grow tax-deferred.

YOUR 401(K) IS A TRAVELING PLAN

You get to keep all your 401(k) plan money—including what your boss contributes (as long as you're vested with the company)—even if you change employers or lose your job. Of course, you can't use your money unless you want to pay taxes and a penalty. To avoid the taxes, you must transfer the money within 60 days to an IRA rollover account or to a plan offered by your new employer. This traveling feature gives the 401(k) plans a big advantage over traditional pension plans which do not allow such transfers unless you are vested in the pension plan. Sometimes, even if you are vested, you will have trouble transferring a pension, but never a 401(k).

- You have a choice of investments—in most cases, at least four, but some plans offer more than a dozen investments.

- You can borrow money from your 401(k) plan without paying a penalty, but you've got to pay back the money (see chapter seven for the ins and outs). The regulations are designed to enable you to get to your funds to meet expenses like helping to finance a house, sending your kids to school, repairing the roof, or paying the doctor bills.

- You can take your 401(k) assets with you if you quit your job or get fired. Note that many plans have vesting rules that affect how long it takes for your company contributions to count.

- You can switch from one investment to another. Unlike an IRA, you don't pay any fee when you move from one investment to another.

- You can use your 401(k) money as collateral for a loan. (Your IRA can't be used as collateral.)

- Your employer might put money into your 401(k) plan. Of course, you've got to participate in the plan for that to happen. You put in $100 and your employer may give you another $100 (free). You pay no taxes on the freebie money until you withdraw it.

- You get to choose how to invest the money that your employer deposits into your account.

- Your employer automatically deducts the money that you want to con-tribute from your paycheck. You tell your employer once, and only once, how much you want deducted—unless you want to increase or decrease the level of your contribution.

- Your employer can't touch your 401(k) money. As a matter of fact, it's a big crime for your employer to fiddle with it at all.

- There are no downsides to 401(k) plans, and you should participate in any that are available to you.

- There is even more information about 401(k) plans in chapter seven.

Pension Plans: It's a '50s Thing

Once upon a time (and oh, what a time it was), most employers in big cities and little towns from sea to shining sea offered their employees pension plans. There are still some companies that offer pension plans, and a few who offer both pension and 401(k) plans. Pension plans are also known as defined-benefit plans.

Typically, with a defined-benefit plan, your employer makes all the contributions to your retirement plan. When you retire, you begin drawing a check each and every month. Every employer uses a slightly different formula for how much that monthly check will be, but every formula consists of three main items:

1. Your average salary. This may be calculated by the five highest salaries you have received, your highest salaries in three out of five years, the average of all your yearly salaries, or some other baseline.

2. The length of time you've been employed.

3. A preset factor or percentage.

The advantage of a pension plan—and this is the major advantage over a 401(k) plan—is that you are guaranteed to get a set amount of money every month no matter how long you live. With a 401(k), there's a possibility your money will run out before you die.

The big plus—the guaranteed monthly income—is offset, though, by some distinct disadvantages. One drawback to a pension plan is that if you die three days after you retire, your pension plan may or may not pay all or a portion of your pension to

COMMON IRA AND 401(K) MISTAKES PART II

Stay away from tax-free bonds when it comes to your retirement account. The interest you earn on tax-free bonds is tax-free, thus the name. Stick this investment in your IRA or 401(k) plan and you are sheltering something that's already sheltered. You're doing something twice (sheltering). Of course, most plans won't even offer this option. But if they do, you'll know to stay away.

your spouse. Another disadvantage is that your company—not you—sets the pension fund policy.

You may also not be eligible—or "vested"—to get your pension unless you stay with the company at least a certain number of years. Moreover, if you quit or get fired, you have to wait until you reach an age—specified by the company—to collect your pension.

If you are covered by a pension plan, ask your employee benefits department to give you the formula for your pension. Also, find out when you were or will be vested.

Can I Set Up My Own IRA If I Have a Pension Plan?

You bet, and that's a good idea, too. Let's say you've got three more years until you vest, but you're getting bad vibes from your employer about your future with the company. You can open an IRA now. You won't be able to deduct your IRA contribution from your taxes, but you will have something for retirement if you get the pink slip next year.

Are you already vested? You should still consider an IRA because your monthly pension check may not cover all your retirement expenses. That's particularly true the longer you live. Your monthly pension will be a fixed amount, but inflation will cut the spending power of that check. Retire at 65 years old with a $1,500 monthly pension, and that $1,500 will be worth only $660 when you are blowing out the candles at your 90th birthday party.

Profit-Sharing Plans

A profit-sharing plan lets you share in the profits of your company. The company, though, decides the percentage of the profits that will be distributed, and your company can change that percentage from year to year. Go ahead and sign up for the plan, but keep in mind that you'll never know how much, or even whether, you are going to get any money in any given year.

The money deposited into your profit-sharing plan by your employer does get invested. Like a pension plan—and unlike a 401(k) plan—you may not be given a choice as to how your money is invested. Don't get twisted about your lack of control. Whatever money you have in your profit-sharing account is a plus, though it probably won't cover even a majority of your retirement expenses.

Self-Employed and Craving

Feeling envious of those drones employed by a company offering a 401(k) plan? No reason to be green, thanks to Eugene Keogh. He's dead, but the retirement plans that carry his name—they were established in 1962 when he was a Congressman from New York—live on.

Keogh felt that self-employed people ought to be able to have their own retirement plans. Today, anyone with self-employment income can establish a Keogh plan. Like a 401(k), the money you contribute into a Keogh plan is deducted off the top of your income. The money you earn on your investments also grows tax-free.

The neat thing about a Keogh is that you can set it up like a 401(k) (you can contribute a set monthly amount) or, if you prefer, like a pension plan. With a defined-contribution Keogh—a cousin of the 401(k)—the amount of money you'll have for your retirement depends on how much you set aside and how savvy you are about investing the money.

A defined-benefit Keogh—a cousin to the pension plan—is more complicated. It's great for someone over the age of 50 who enjoys a high income level and who wants to shelter a lot of that money from Mr. Taxman.

CALCULATING THE RATE OF RETURN

If your calculator isn't handy, your sixth-grade math will suffice to let you determine the rate of return for your investments. The **higher the rate,** the harder your investments are working for you.

$(N - Y)/T$ = Rate of Return

N = Value of your investment now

Y = Value of your investment when you bought it

T = Time you held the investment. T is always calculated in years. If you hold an investment for ten years and three months, T equals 10.25 years.

Here's how a defined-benefit Keogh works. Let's say you had a self-employment income of $50,000 in 1994, $40,000 in 1995, and $66,000 in 1996. Your average income for those three years was $52,000.

How much can you set aside in this type of Keogh? Whatever it takes to fund a benefit of $52,000 each year of your retirement. If you are 57 years old and want to retire at age 67, you'll have to make some pretty big contributions each year until you are 67 to get to that level. At age 27, you have 40 years to fund your retirement account, so you won't be required to put in as much. Get some expert advice if you are considering a defined-benefit Keogh. There are lots of exceptions that can trip you up.

You can consult with a tax lawyer or a financial planner. For a list of Certified Financial Planners in your area, call (800) 282-PLAN. You will receive up to three experts in your area along with profiles and information on how to get in touch with them.

Why Your 401(k) Is Better than Your IRA for Retirement Investing

- You can contribute more: $9,500 to a 401(k) versus $2,000 to your IRA

- You pay less in taxes: again, it's $9,500 versus $2,000

- You pay no fees for switching from one investment to another

- You can borrow from it for lots of things

- You don't have to remember to contribute once you've signed on. You can be an investment couch potato. It's your employer's responsibility—not yours—to automatically make the specified deductions from your paycheck.

Just Do It!

You've got good choices in the type of retirement accounts that are best for you. Delay taking action and you'll miss the chance to make your savings compound.

You know now what you can do about saving, about investing, and about retirement accounts for your investments. Don't think about it, just do it!

THE *three* amigos *in your* POCKET

Life without friends would be a pretty dismal existence. Hopefully, that's not your plight. You've probably got lots of **friends** whose company you enjoy and maybe you also have a few very special and important ones who see you through the tough times and make the happy moments truly **joyous.**

Now, get acquainted with the three amigos who will help you fashion your retirement plan, guiding your decisions to keep it strong and healthy. These three concepts—asset allocation, diversification, and leverage—will help you when the financial markets soar and when they take a tailspin. They also will provide the framework for the many investment decisions you will make between now and when you retire. And you will depend on them after you retire to make your investments last all through your retirement years.

There are other investment concepts and techniques you'll rely upon (see chapter ten), but the three amigos are the ones who will give you the retirement you deserve.

WHY NOT 100 PERCENT EQUITIES?

Equities are volatile—they go up and down faster than **fixed-rate** investments. Thus, a stock market crash can wipe out a portion of your retirement savings. Not a problem when you are young, but it is a big problem as you get closer to retiring.

Let's say the stock market declines 10 percent over a couple of days just before you are set to retire. It then stays in the doldrums for the next two and a half years. Your rock-and-hard-place choice will be between waiting a couple of years for the market—and your investments—to recover or merely settling for less **retirement money.** Fixed-income investments can help to offset equity declines.

Asset Allocation Gardening

How you divide your investments—between stocks and bonds, equity and debt, and low rate of return and high rate of return—is the single most important concept for building a secure retirement plan. It's more important than the individual stock funds or bond funds you choose.

Picking the right mix of investments is much like landscaping the property on which your home sits. Wise gardeners plant a mix of slow-growing evergreens and fast-growing, luscious-colored perennials such as azaleas, roses, and hydrangeas.

Achieving your long-term financial goals also means planting different types of investments in your retirement plan. Don't make the mistake of putting all your money into what may appear to be conservative investments, such as low-rate-of-return CDs or money market funds. That approach can create less financial security than dividing your money between equities and some fixed-income investments. Over the years you need different types of investments to reach your goal. And you need them in different proportions.

Your retirement investments are for your long-term financial security. Don't invest your retirement money as if you will be using or needing those funds in 30 days or even a year. Checking accounts and money market funds which are outside your retirement plan are designed for that.

A Simple Rule

There is a very simple rule you can use for creating your financial landscape. Just take your age and subtract it from 100. That will give you the rock-bottom minimum percentage of money you should invest in equities. The remaining percentage can go into bonds, bond funds, and other fixed-income investments.

RETURN RATES

Average Annual Rates of Return Over the Past 50 Years

Aggressive Growth
Stocks   12.0%

Growth & Income
Stocks   10.0%

Bonds   5.5%

This is called asset allocation because you have allocated, or distributed, your assets among different investment types in your retirement plan. Take a look at how asset allocation works as you grow older.

Age	% Equities	% Fixed-Income
25	75	25
35	65	35
45	55	45
55	45	55
65	35	65

Thus, at 25 years old, at the very least, 75 percent of your savings can go into equities and up to 25 percent into fixed-income or debt vehicles. At age 45, you put 55 percent of your investments into equities. Even at the retirement age of 65, some 35 percent of your investments still can be in equities.

Follow the Formula, Not the Markets

Stick with the asset allocation formula and you need not worry about which direction the stock market or bond market is heading. You shouldn't even try to guess. That's called market timing, and trying to do it can lead to disaster.

The long-term behavior of the financial markets shows that allocating your investments properly is a better route to financial security than trying to figure out whether equities will be zooming higher or lower in the short term. That's because over the long term—which is your horizon for investing for retirement—equities have historically performed better than any other type of investment.

Of course, equities tend to rise and fall faster over the short term than low-yielding fixed-income vehicles. Thus, as you near retirement, you can put more money into fixed-income investments and less into equities which can be more volatile.

The Why of Asset Allocation

When you follow your asset allocation amigo you take the biggest investment risks when you are young, so that any mistakes or missteps can be corrected as you grow older. The bigger risks also translate into bigger returns, and that means more money for you when you retire.

Asset allocation also provides an investing framework that is easy to follow. At age 30, you might be tempted to put a lot of money into bonds because they happened to perform better than stocks over the past three years. That may be true for a particular short-term period, but over the long term, stocks will do better than bonds.

Divide and Conquer

Look at what investing with and without the asset allocation amigo can mean. Both Jennifer and Bernie invest their retirement savings in a tax-deferred account such as an IRA or 401(k) plan. Both struggle to save $2,000, but take a different approach for investing their savings.

Jennifer ignores the asset allocation amigo. She thinks she will be "conservative" with her investments. Starting at age 25, she puts $2,000 every year into her retirement plan. For 40 years, she puts all her money into fixed-income, low-yielding investments which return only 3 percent after inflation.

Jennifer's Retirement Plan: Without the Asset Allocation Amigo

Age	Equity% at 6% interest	Fixed-Income% at 3% interest
25	0	100
35	0	100
45	0	100
55	0	100
65	0	100

Bernie also saves $2,000 each year and very wisely invests with asset allocation in mind. At age 25, he puts 75 percent of his investments into equities and 25 percent into fixed-income vehicles. Every ten years, he changes his investment mix. Thus, at age 35, he begins to put only 65 percent into equities. His equity investments earn him—on average—6 percent a year.

Bernie's Retirement Plan: With the Asset Allocation Amigo

Age	Equity% at 6% interest	Fixed-Income% at 3% interest
25	75	25
35	65	35
45	55	45
55	45	55
65	35	65

After 40 years, Jennifer and Bernie are ready to retire and enjoy the fruits of their savings. But conservatively inclined Jennifer has only $155,326 in her plan. By investing in both equities and in fixed-income vehicles such as bond funds, Bernie amasses $437,286. That difference keeps Jennifer pinching pennies during retirement while Bernie sails through his retirement in a 45-foot sailboat.

Jennifer's Asset Allocation Penalty

Age	Equity%	Fixed-Income%	Value Retirement Plan
25	0	100	$ 2,000
35	0	100	23,615
45	0	100	55,325
55	0	100	98,005
65	0	100	155,326

Bernie's Asset Allocation Reward

Age	Equity%	Fixed-Income%	Value of Retirement Plan
25	75	25	$ 2,000
35	65	35	30,850
45	55	45	93,618
55	45	55	216,549
65	35	65	437,286

Stick with the asset allocation amigo when you invest for retirement. It gives you an easy framework for investing and can make the difference between a bare-bones retirement existence and a very comfortable one.

Your Diversification Amigo

Once you've bonded with your asset allocation amigo, you'll want to start spending some time with your diversification friend, too.

Diversification's nickname is "spreading-it-around." Diversification also follows that old saw, "Don't put all your eggs in one basket."

Translating groceries to investments, that means don't tie your entire investment plan to your employer even if your employer does offer a terrific 401(k) or profit-sharing plan. It means buying more than one type of equity or fixed-income investment. It means having both liquid and illiquid assets. By diversifying, your entire retirement plan will not be scuttled if one aspect of the plan hits a snag.

Diversify Your Investment Landscape

Let's return to the landscaping analogy to understand the rewards of diversification and the penalties when it is ignored. Picture, if you will, two identical homes on a plot in Anytown, America. Stacy and Antoine Rockford choose to frame their home with hundreds of azalea plants. Every spring the plants bloom in an ever-larger burst of luscious color.

Claire and Matthew Berger take a different landscaping tack. They plant some deciduous trees, some evergreen trees and shrubs, and some perennial flowers and bushes, including two azaleas. All year, their greenery grows and flourishes, although some plants grow faster than others and their property is less renowned in the neighborhood for its springtime abundance.

Weather the Storm

Years pass and both the Rockfords and Bergers are ready to retire and sell their homes. Unfortunately, in late spring when the For Sale signs are erected on both properties, a curious weather pattern materializes which creates extended and severe subzero cold dubbed by the media as "The Storm of the Century."

All the azaleas that the Rockfords lovingly planted die, making their property resemble Bosnia at its worst. The Berger property still looks appealing. The two withered azalea plants are hardly noticed among the other diverse greenery and flowers.

Claire and Matthew Berger quickly discard the two azaleas, promptly sell their home, and close the deal on their new lakeside retirement house.

THE COMPANY LINE

Your Company-Sponsored Plan versus Your Company Stock

That company-sponsored retirement plan is a great deal. Be careful, though, about putting too much money into the stock of the company for which you work. If disaster befalls your company, the stock may plummet. On top of that, you may lose your job, which will make saving for retirement more difficult. Spread your risk around. Go light on the company stock.

Meanwhile, the Rockfords are stuck in the old home. They can either take a reduced price for their property or pay to have all the blighted azaleas removed and new greenery put in its place. In either case, they discover the delay means they miss the opportunity to buy the retirement home they also wanted by the lake.

Diversify your plan and you will find your financial flora will flourish over the years. Ignore your diversification friend and your retirement plan can become a blighted eyesore. To landscape your financial future, you should remember to plant your investments in a diverse way.

IT'S ALL IN THE TIMING

The Long, Short, and Intermediate of It

The world of fixed-income investments defines those investments according to how long you keep them until they stop earning income for you. That's the maturity of a fixed-income investment. Here's how the maturities are defined:

Short-Term: Anything less than three years.

Intermediate-Term: Three to seven years.

Long-Term: Anything more than seven years.

Diversify Your Risks for a Big Reward

Spreading your investments among a number of different types of equities and debt vehicles like bond funds protects you against various scenarios or risks. There are different types of risk just as there are numerous weather patterns, pests, and diseases that can attack the trees, shrubs, and flowers on your property.

High inflation and spiraling interest rates can make your investment in bonds decline. Deflation can lower the value of a real estate investment below the amount of equity you have in that property. That can create a situation where you may owe more to the bank than you could get for the property if you sold it.

A change in government policy—regarding health care or the environment, for instance—can devastate your investment in an individual company or in a number of stocks within one industry. Market risk exists, too. For instance, thousands of individual stocks can take a massive dive all at the same time, just as they did in October 1987 and 1989. Thus, you should never plant too much of your money in any one investment.

Diversify Fixed-Income Investments

Your fixed-income investments provide a steady flow of income, but the value of those investments declines as interest rates rise and, conversely, the value moves higher when interest rates fall. Corporate and U.S. government bonds, bond funds, and fixed annuities fall into this category.

To reduce your interest rate risk, purchase different types of bonds and bond funds. A good mix is some corporate bonds and some U.S. government bonds. Within each category, you'll want long-term bonds and medium-term bonds—also known as intermediate bonds—because interest rate changes can impact long- and medium-term bonds in a slightly different way. For example, a rise in interest rates can lower the value of your short-term bonds a lot less than it does your long-term bonds.

Diversify Your Equities

It's especially important to diversify your equity investments. Owning stocks and mutual funds is key to growing any diversified retirement portfolio because over the long term, stocks have performed better than any other type of investment. But over the short term of a year or two, the value of one type of equity can rise or fall to a greater degree than another type.

MAKE YOUR EMPLOYER PAY

Take **advantage** of every financial opportunity your employer provides:

• Join the employee retirement plans.

• Use any **benefits** that pay for or let you borrow to take educational courses.

• Study the investment materials your employer gives you. Carefully listen to any and all investment seminars your employer offers.

• Ask if your employer will match a **charitable** contribution you make.

• File your **expense report** sooner rather than later.

You should diversify your equities among income, growth, and the combination growth-and-income vehicles. You can buy individual stocks that are designed for growth, for income, or for both income and growth. You can buy mutual funds that are designed to act like an income stock or a growth-and-income stock.

Some portion of your investments should be in international stocks as well. There are plenty of mutual funds that invest in companies that do business internationally or that invest in overseas companies. Mutual funds that invest in the equities of just one country also exist.

Investing in mutual funds is a great way to spread your risk because mutual funds invest in a number of different stocks. A decline in an individual stock can be cushioned by the uptick in another.

Keep Your Leverage Amigo Close

Your third and final best investment friend is leverage, a Tom Sawyer kind of fellow. Remember how Tom got his friends to paint the fence for him? Your friend leverage gets you help painting your investment fence.

Leverage means letting someone else or some investment loophole work for you. Leverage is a tax-deferred account. Leverage is a 401(k) plan where your employer kicks in money to you. Leverage is compounding. Leverage is that free investment seminar you were invited to by that snazzy brokerage firm. Go to the seminar. You don't have to buy from the firm.

Smart investors know how to take advantage of a drop in the equity and debt markets. They continue to buy. Foolish investors panic. They sell. If you invest a small amount of money on a regular and consistent basis, you can let declines in the stock market work to your advantage by using dollar cost averaging, a truly cool leveraging concept.

One of the dumbest moves you can make is to buy at the top of the market when debt or equity prices are at their highest and then to sell—or just not buy—at the bottom of the market when those prices fall. Unfortunately, many investors commit this egregious sin of investing.

Be smart. Invest a little money every pay period—in sunny times when the markets are rising and in stormy times when the markets fall. Over an extended period of time, you'll spend less money for each equity share than the person who makes one big lump-sum investment or who buys equity shares only when the market is climbing higher. This also means you end up with more shares of a stock or mutual fund. Best of all, this investing concept, called dollar cost averaging, works for both your equity and debt investments.

How Dollar Cost Averaging Works

Dollar cost averaging allows you to take advantage of stock market fluctuations. Rather than purchasing your stock all at one time, you purchase a little at a time, over a long period of time. You'll never be able to predict the future and pinpoint the exact time when the stock you want to buy is at its lowest point. With dollar cost averaging, the price at which you purchase the stock averages out over the long run, you will most likely end up with a lower price than if you had purchased all your shares at once.

Look at how you can leverage your investments with dollar cost averaging. Emilio ignores the dollar cost averaging strategy. He has $5,000 and he invests all of that in one lump sum in an equity mutual fund. The fund's shares sell for $10 each, so Emilio buys 500 shares.

During a ten-month period, the price of those shares rises some months, falls in others. At the end of the period, the price of the shares is still $10 and Emilio still has 500 shares.

Catherine invests $500 every month when she gets her paycheck or turns the investing over to her 401(k) plan. That steady strategy gives her an investing advantage over Emilio.

Emilio

Month	Share Price	$ Invested	# Shares Bought
1 & 2	$10	$5,000	100
3 & 4	12	none	none
5 & 6	8	none	none
7 & 8	6	none	none
9 & 10	10	none	none

Total shares bought for $5,000 = 100 at average cost of $10 a share

Catherine

Month	Share Price	$ Invested	# Shares Bought
1 & 2	$10	$500	100.0
3 & 4	12	500	83.3
5 & 6	8	500	125.0
7 & 8	6	500	166.7
9 & 10	10	500	100.0

Total shares bought for $5,000 = 575 at average cost of $8.69 a share

Catherine got more bang—more shares—for her $5,000 total investment than Emilio did, thanks to dollar cost averaging. Catherine let price declines work for her. Emilio spent many sleepless nights worrying about whether he should sell his equity shares.

Make investing easy for you to do. Invest a little, but regularly and consistently, so you can get dollar cost averaging to leverage your savings.

Stick with Your Friends

Your three amigos—asset allocation, diversification, and leverage—make investing easy. Don't abandon them when the financial markets decline or when your cousin Joey advises you to put all your money into a great bond fund or your colleague gives you a stock tip on a great new start-up firm.

Those investments may be good but not for all your retirement assets. Be true to your three amigos and they will deliver for you.

HOW THE 401(k) plan works 4-U

CHAPTER SEVEN

A *401(k) can be the single best retirement savings vehicle for you. Saving is* **painless** *because you never get your hands on the money. You can take your funds with you if you leave your job. Your* **boss** *may kick money into your account and you can borrow from your account. The catch? You* **DO** *have to participate.*

In addition to the advantages listed earlier, having a 401(k) plan means you get to pay taxes on lower income figures and your earnings grow tax-deferred. The consistent and regular contributions also let you take advantage of dollar cost averaging. What's the catch? Your employer has to offer a 401(k) option, and YOU have to participate.

But it's all so easy. You don't need to fiddle with opening an account. You also don't have to pay a bank, brokerage firm, or mutual fund any fees to maintain your account. Your employer does all the record keeping. You just have to file the paper into a folder.

Your employer is obligated to furnish you with information about your investments. Many employers also provide newsletters that give you investing tips for your 401(k) plan.

You don't have to manage your own money except to decide the asset allocation. Through an investment adviser, your employer offers you different investment funds that are appropriate for retirement savings. The investment adviser is paid to pick the best funds so you don't have to choose from among the thousands of mutual funds out there in investment land.

You can switch your investments from fund to fund without paying a dime. This makes it easy to rejigger your retirement account, according to the asset allocation rule, as you grow older.

Using Other People's Money

The biggest bang you can get from your 401(k) is the match that most employers make to your contributions. This is free money. Better still, the money contributed is tax-deferred—as is the interest it earns.

Take a look at the advantages of investing with a 401(k) plan. Courtney and Richard are saving for retirement years. Both invest $2,000 a year, earn 5 percent on average on their investment, and are in the 28 percent tax bracket. But Courtney saves through a 401(k) plan. Richard establishes his own savings plan with a broker to whom he must pay fees.

Courtney's employer matches each dollar she invests with another 50 cents. In year one, Courtney contributes $2,000 and her employer matches that with $1,000. At the end of the year, Courtney has $3,000 plus the 5 percent, or $150, she earned on that money for a total of $3,150.

Richard also earned 5 percent. But his total investment was only $2,000 so he earns only $100. And Richard must pay $28 in taxes on the $100 he earned. That leaves him only $2,072 to reinvest.

In year two, Courtney gets another $3,150 added to her account. Meanwhile, her first year's investment of $3,150 also earns $157.50. Her total account is $6,457.50 at the end of year two. Richard is not doing so well. He has earned only $74.59 after taxes on his carried-over investment plus $72 after taxes on his current-year investment of $2,000. His total at the end of year two is $4,218.59.

Year after year, Courtney's savings expand. Richard's do, too, but not as much. He may pay taxes on his investment earnings once he sells (depending on whether or not he sells to realize gains), gets nothing from his employer, and must pay his broker fees to invest his money. He devotes a couple hours every week to keep abreast of fast-breaking financial news. He even has subscribed to a newsletter for $100 a year to help him with his investment plan.

Courtney's reward for using other people's money is that she has almost twice as much saved for retirement as Richard.

Courtney's 401(k) Retirement Account

End of Year #	Total Contribution	Contrib. + Carryover	Income	Total
1	$3,000.00	$ 0.00	$ 150.00	$3,150.00
2	3,000.00	6,150.00	307.50	6,457.50
3	3,000.00	9,457.50	472.88	9,930.38
4	3,000.00	12,930.38	646.52	13,576.89
5	3,000.00	16,576.89	828.84	17,405.74
6	3,000.00	20,405.74	1,020.29	21,426.03
7	3,000.00	24,426.03	1,221.30	25,647.33
8	3,000.00	28,647.33	1,432.37	30,079.69
9	3,000.00	33,079.69	1,653.98	34,733.68
10	3,000.00	37,733.68	1,886.68	39,620.36
11	3,000.00	42,620.36	2,131.02	44,751.38
12	3,000.00	47,751.38	2,387.57	50,138.95
13	3,000.00	53,138.95	2,656.95	55,795.90
14	3,000.00	58,795.90	2,939.79	61,735.69
15	3,000.00	64,735.69	3,236.78	67,972.48
16	3,000.00	70,972.48	3,548.62	74,521.10

17	3,000.00	77,521.10	3,876.05	81,397.15
18	3,000.00	84,397.15	4,219.86	88,617.01
19	3,000.00	91,617.01	4,580.85	96,197.86
20	3,000.00	99,197.86	4,959.89	104,157.76

Richard's Retirement Account

End of Year #	Total Contribution	Contrib. + Carryover	Income before taxes	Reduction	Total
1	$2,000.00	$ 0.00	$ 100.00	$ 72.00	$ 2,072.00
2	2,000.00	4.072.00	203.60	146.59	4,218.59
3	2,000.00	6,218.59	310.93	223.87	6,442.46
4	2,000.00	8,442.46	422.12	303.93	8,746.39
5	2,000.00	10,746.39	537.32	386.87	11,133.26
6	2,000.00	13,133.26	656.66	472.80	13,606.06
7	2,000.00	15,606.06	780.30	561.82	16,167.88
8	2,000.00	18,167.88	908.39	654.04	18,821.92
9	2,000.00	20,821.92	1,041.10	749.59	21,571.51
10	2,000.00	23,571.51	1,178.58	848.57	24,420.08
11	2,000.00	26,420.08	1,321.00	951.12	27,371.21
12	2,000.00	29,371.21	1,468.56	1,057.36	30,428.57
13	2,000.00	32,428.57	1,621.43	1,167.43	33,596.00
14	2,000.00	35,596.00	1,779.80	1,281.46	36,877.45
15	2,000.00	38,877.45	1,943.87	1,399.59	40,277.04
16	2,000.00	42,277.04	2,113.85	1,521.97	43,799.01
17	2,000.00	45,799.01	2,289.95	1,648.76	47,447.78
18	2,000.00	49,447.78	2,472.39	1,780.12	51,227.90
19	2,000.00	53,227.90	2,661.39	1,916.20	55,144.10
20	2,000.00	57,144.10	2,857.21	2,057.19	59,201.29

Totals are before brokerage fees, which Richard must pay and Courtney does not.

Your 401(k) Borrowing Power

Borrowing from your 401(k) plan is ridiculously easy. So easy that you may be tempted to dip into your retirement account for expensive holiday gifts or for a luxury sports car. Refrain from that. Borrowing from your 401(k) is just like borrowing from a bank. You'll need to pay the loan back with interest.

But you might consider borrowing to pay for your child's college education or for that mouthful of orthodontic work. You should consider paying off high credit card balances with your 401(k) money, because the interest you are being charged on your credit cards is higher than the interest you will pay back to yourself with a 401(k) loan.

Four out of five 401(k) plans permit you to borrow from your own account. Pay back the loan and you incur no tax penalty. It's a pretty good deal.

Borrowing a little from your 401(k) will reduce your retirement funds only marginally if you pay back the loan and continue to let your savings grow tax-free. Look how much is lost—not much—if you need to borrow from your fund.

Raul and Deirdre each have $40,000 in their 401(k) accounts. At age 35, both let their investments sit—they decide not to save any more through their account. Assume that their investments—which just sit—earn 10 percent over the next 30 years until they each want to retire at age 65.

Over that 30-year period, the cost to Deirdre to borrow $10,000 from her 401(k) plan is only $5,000.

Raul's 401(k) Account
Age 35 Now: $40,000

Plan grows at 10 percent, compounded, for 30 years
Age 65 in 30 years: $698,000

Deirdre's 401(k) Account
Age 35 Now: $40,000

$10,000 loan at 7 percent
Pays back loan in five years plus $2,200 interest

Plan grows at 10 percent compounded, for 30 years
Age 65 in 30 years: $693,000

The difference between the two accounts is only $5,000. In effect, Deirdre borrowed $10,000, but only paid back $5,000.

Cutting the Risk/Reward Tradeoff with Your 401(k)

Here's how a lower return—and thus lower risk—earns you the same as a higher return in a taxable account. The difference is taxes, which are deferred in a 401(k) plan.

	Tax-Deferred Account	Regular Account
Return on $10,000	at 6% = $600	at 8.3% = $830
Taxes at 28%	$0	$232
Return after Taxes	$600	$598
YOU KEEP	$600	$598
Equivalent Return	6.00%	5.98%

Saving for Your Child's College Education with Your 401(k)

The choice is seemingly confounding. Given your limited financial resources, should you save for your own retirement years or focus on accumulating money for your children's college education? Faced with such an emotionally conflicting choice, your first response is to put your children first. "I'll worry about my retirement finances after the kids graduate," you might think.

While such unselfish sentiments are admirable, a children-first saving strategy not only can put your financial security in jeopardy, but it may prove counterproductive to reaching the college goal.

With your 401(k), you can have your cake and eat it, too: you can finance a college education and save for your own retirement. To do that, though, you must save for your retirement first. Only then are you apt to have the financial resources that provide some appealing options to pay those hefty college bills.

This strategy hinges upon saving as much as possible through your 401(k) so you'll have the money you need when your children begin obsessing about their SAT and ACT scores and college admissions applications. With a substantial retirement fund amassed, you can temporarily suspend your contributions to your 401(k) plan. Your investments, of course, continue to compound. You can then apply the money you would have invested toward the college bills. Thus, you pay the college bills as if you were paying yourself in your 401(k).

Take a look. Let's say you've been contributing to your 401(k) for 15 years and your account boasts over $100,000. With some money saved for retirement, you might lower or even suspend your 401(k) contribution which stands at $4,000 a year. Over the next four years, you can focus on those education bills. Suspending your 401(k) contributions of $4,000 will give you an extra $2,880 a year after taxes in the 28 percent bracket.

But most likely, you still will face a shortfall. At this point, you probably will be eyeing some type of financial aid package. Here is where the wisdom of your 401(k) investing really comes into play.

To qualify for financial aid, you must detail your financial resources—your bank deposits, your money market funds, your equities, and your bond holdings. These will be viewed as current assets even if you intend to use the money for your retirement. The more assets you have, the less financial aid you'll get.

However, your 401(k) money is not counted by the college financial aid officers. That means you can qualify for a bigger financial aid package.

The final but sweetest twist to this strategy is that you may be able to borrow from your 401(k) plan to pay the college bills. Of course, you must pay back the 401(k) with interest and strictly adhere to the payback schedule. Here's another goody: The interest you pay the 401(k) plan goes back to you.

While the borrowing option is available with all 401(k) plans, you are limited to withdrawing no more than—perhaps less than—50 percent of your funds in the plan. Explore how much your 401(k) will let you borrow. It may be the best way to finance your children's college education. Your employee benefits department can provide this information and can explain the procedure for borrowing from your 401(k) plan.

Get Bigger Returns with Smaller Risk

To grow your retirement investments, you want to get the highest return for the smallest amount of risk possible. But risk and return are linked. The lower the risk, the lower the return. There is a way around this trade-off: your 401(k).

Because your 401(k) is tax-deferred, the actual return you get will be higher than the return you achieve in a regular account. Thus, with your 401(k), you can either get:

- A higher return for a lower equivalent risk than in a regular account

- A lower risk for a higher equivalent return than in a regular account

The historical returns of aggressive growth stocks and of growth and income stocks are:

- Aggressive growth stocks: 12 percent with greater risk

- Growth and income stocks: 10 percent with less risk

Are You Part of the Rising Trend Line?

The number of people enjoying the advantages of investing through a 401(k) plan more than doubled over the past decade.

Moreover, the ranks of 401(k) investors are forecast to continue to expand as more and more people recognize the financial advantages of saving for retirement in this tax-deferred account, in bull markets and bear markets alike.

Number of participants (in millions)	Year
10.8	1986
13.7	1988
15.6	1990
18.5	1992
20.9	1994
23.8	1996
26.7	1998 (Projected)
29.6	2000 (Projected)

Source: Access Research, Inc., Windsor, CT

Invest through a 401(k) and you get an equivalent 12 percent return investing in growth and income stocks. All you've given up is the risk, not the return.

Most tax-deferred investments return either a 6 percent, 8 percent or, at the most, a 10 percent return on average. If you invest your money in a taxable investment, you will need to achieve a higher rate of return in order to end up with the same amount of money once you are ready to retire. The table below shows you how much more of a return you will need depending upon your tax bracket.

Return from Tax-Deferred Plan	6.0%	8.0%	10.0%
Tax Bracket	**Return Needed for Taxable Fund to Match Return of Tax-Deferred Plan**		
15.0%	7.1%	9.4%	11.8%
28.0%	8.3%	11.1%	13.9%

Your Very Portable 401(k)

Millions of people leave their jobs each year. Companies fold and have to fire all their workers. Mergers produce pink slips. A job relocation for your spouse means one for you, too, or you may be the one who gets that attractive job offer halfway across the continent.

You can move your 401(k) plan a lot more easily than you can move your household belongings. Your 401(k) is also more transportable than a traditional pension plan, which may evaporate unless you qualify under some magic formula of age plus years of working for the company.

Your Transfer Choices

If you have more than $3,500 in your 401(k) plan, you may have as many as three different moving options:

1. You can leave the money in your former company's plan.

2. You may be able to transfer your 401(k) plan money into your new employer's plan.

3. You can transfer or roll over your money into an IRA.

What you don't want to do is to take your 401(k) money and spend it. You'll get hit with a huge tax penalty.

Stay with the Old or Go with the New?

Do a little investigating before you decide whether you want to leave your money in the old plan or transfer to a new 401(k) plan. Look at the investment offerings and borrowing features of both plans.

Look at which plan offers you the most investment choices. You should also compare how those investment offerings have performed.

Borrow Here or Borrow There?

If you have borrowed from your old plan, you may have to repay the loan to yourself before you can transfer the money. Also, check to see whether your old plan will allow you to borrow in the future, even after you've left the company. Some plans do. See what the new plan offers in terms of borrowing power. Some plans allow you to borrow up to 50 percent, while others put a lower cap on your borrowing level.

RAW LAND—A RAW DEAL

A word of warning: Buying raw land is a highly speculative investment and one which most people should avoid. It's hard to determine the resale value of land that has not been developed. That makes it extremely difficult to find a buyer. Worse still, you will have to pay property taxes even though you get no income from the land.

Don't Think about It. Jump!

If you participate in a 401(k) plan, all these terrific benefits are yours. Almost every large employer has a 401(k) plan. Many small companies offer 401(k)s as alternatives to traditional pension funds.

Over 20 million Americans are enjoying the benefits of these very flexible plans. This is a group you, too, want to join. So, just sign up, sit back, and watch your retirement savings grow.

DIVERSIFY
diversify
and
diversify
SOME MORE!

CHAPTER EIGHT

Buying a home and purchasing insurance may fit into your retirement savings plan. **Know** the advantages and drawbacks of these investment vehicles. Choose the pieces that will make the retirement **movie** you are directing an **award-winning one.**

The ability to buy a home is ingrained in the American Dream. Owning a home gives you an emotional sense of belonging to the community. Owning a home gives you tax advantages because you can deduct your mortgage interest and your property taxes. Owning a home can be a good investment. But before you take the plunge, carefully consider whether or not it fits into your retirement plan.

When you weigh the advantages and disadvantages of home ownership, a lot of different factors come into play—many of them dependent on your individual situation. Buying a home is like a forced savings plan. While some people may forgo making a contribution to a retirement savings plan, most people won't take a chance missing a mortgage payment and risk having the mortgage company ask for immediate repayment or, at worst, foreclosure.

Home Ownership May Not Be Best for You

Don't jump to the conclusion, though, that the only avenue to retirement financial security is through home ownership. If your job or your spouse's job transfers you every couple of years from one city to the next, buying a home may prove to be a burden. If you rent out your home, you'll have to find your own tenant, pay for a thorough credit check, and then maintain the property from far away.

Selling a home every couple of years eats away at price appreciation. As a seller, you will have to pay fees to a real estate broker (if you use one). You may also have to spend some money to get your house "in shape" for the prospective buyers who come through to see it.

Once you sell a house, you have to reinvest any profits into another home within a limited period of time (currently two years). The penalty for just taking the profits is a 28 percent capital gains tax. And as a buyer, you've got title insurance, mortgage points, and a host of other charges.

Consider Other Real Estate Investments

Some of your retirement savings should be in real estate. You don't have to own a home, though, to get this real estate component of your retirement plan. You can buy mutual funds that invest in real estate, or you can buy a real estate investment trust (REIT). In a REIT, you pool your money with other investors and the pooled money buys real estate property. Like mutual funds, REITs are publicly traded on stock exchanges.

There are two types of REITs in which you can invest. Equity REITs buy real estate and then you, as an investor, receive the income from the properties. You may also receive a payment if a property in the REIT is sold. Other REITs specialize in lending money to building developers. With these mortgage REITs, you receive the interest the developers pay on the loans you've made to them.

Get Qualified Before You Buy

Still itching for a home of your own? First, get prequalified. Go to a bank, savings and loan, or a mortgage banker and find out if you qualify for a mortgage and how big a mortgage you can get.

That will help you limit the possibilities when you start looking for a home. It will also cut the disappointment if you find something you really can't afford. Nothing is worse than hunting for a house, finding the perfect home, and then discovering the home is way out of your reach because you don't come close to getting a mortgage big enough to finance the purchase price.

There's another big advantage to getting prequalified. A seller may be more inclined to accept your buy offer over an offer by someone who is not prequalified. The seller knows you are able to get a mortgage and that your offer is reliable.

RISING VALUE

See How a $100,000 Home Rises in Value at Different Appreciation Rates

Even modest price appreciation each year can boost the value of your home over the long term. At a 4 percent annual appreciation rate, a $100,000 home will be worth $148,024 in ten years.

This table shows the value of a $100,000 house after ten years given a certain annual appreciation rate.

Rate	Value
2%	$121,899
3%	$134,392
4%	$148,024
5%	$162,889
6%	$179,085
7%	$196,715
8%	$215,893
9%	$236,736
10%	$259,374

Bridal Registry Accounts

Getting married but not looking forward to all those pots and pans, ice buckets, and picnic baskets? Would you rather get money put into an account designed to accumulate a down payment for your first home? Probably.

Well, Uncle Sam wants to help you do just that. In late 1996, the government established the Bridal Registry Accounts program. Banks and savings and loan institutions approved by the Federal Housing Administration now offer these accounts. Establish an account, and willing gift givers can deposit money toward a home for you into the account. The interest you get on the account will be low, but FHA-approved mortgages require as little as a 3 percent down payment.

The catch is that the FHA limits the size of the mortgage it will under-write to $157,000. That may not get you far if you live in places like Manhattan or San Francisco. For everyone else, it wouldn't hurt to check it out.

It's Still Location, Location, Location

It's a cliché, but one which you should commit to memory. The community in which you buy a home is the single most important factor which determines whether your home will increase in value rapidly, or modestly, or if it will decline.

The second rule of thumb is to buy the most inexpensive home in the best neighborhood. If your home is the most expensive home in the area, it probably will not rise in value as much as the smaller home down the street.

Dealing with Real Estate Agents

The first thing you must realize when you look for a house is that you probably can't avoid a real estate agent. The second thing to remember is that the seller pays the agent, which means that the agent is, in effect, working for the seller. The agent only gets paid, though, if you and the seller agree on a price. Thus, it is in the agent's best interest to get the seller to come down in price and to get you to go up in price, so the two of you meet and the agent can collect a commission.

Don't let an agent talk you into buying a house that is too expensive for your budget. You'll hear a lot about how your home is a great investment. But a home that's a big financial stretch for you can scuttle any hope you have for putting away other money for your retirement. Know what you can afford and stand your ground firmly.

It's your money, your debt, and your retirement savings plan that's at stake. The agent won't be there to take care of you in your retirement years.

How Do You Know When the Real Estate Market Is at Its Low Point?

As with any investment, you want to buy as close to the bottom and sell as close to the top as possible. It's never a sure thing, but the market is close to bottom when price declines are widespread. Two signs that the market is getting ready to go up are falling interest rates nationally and rising employment locally. The number of homes sold will also rise before the prices of those homes increase. Such a buying opportunity can last 12 to 18 months.

What Kind of Rate of Return Can You Expect on Your Home?

The big price escalations of the 1970s and 1980s were fueled by high inflation, nesting baby boomers, and speculation. That was the historical exception.

You can expect the price appreciation on a home or condo you buy to be lower than in those boom times, but still good. Home prices should beat inflation by a point or two, rising an average of 5 percent to 5.5 percent a year.

A Home versus Stocks: Compare the Rates of Return

The rate of return on your home depends on the price increase, the interest you pay on your mortgage, and the size of your down payment. Assume the price rises 4 percent each year, your mortgage rate is 10 percent, and you put down 20 percent. Your rate of return would be 10.4 percent.

That's a little more than the 10 percent annual historical return for growth and income stocks, but less than the 12 percent return on aggressive growth stocks.

Why Not Put All Your Retirement Assets into Real Estate?

Do that and you abandon two of your investment amigos—asset allocation and diversification. Your home appreciates in value over the long term, but it is an illiquid asset. Putting all your money into a home with a 30-year mortgage is akin to putting all your retirement savings into 30-year bonds issued by just one company.

You also certainly wouldn't put all your investments into nineteenth-century English landscape paintings, so why put it all into a home, which can be just as hard to sell?

Does Remodeling Pay?

Do you already own a home, but wonder how a remodeling project might increase the value of your home? Check to see if the money you spend for that remodeling will translate into a higher resale value of your home. Notice that $10,000 spent for a backyard pool raises the value of your home by only $4,600, but a $10,000 bathroom ups your home value by an equal amount.

Remodeling Project	% You Get Back When You Sell Your Home
Full Bathroom	100
Fireplace	85
Deck	82
Kitchen	74
Additional Room	69
Pool	46

These are general guidelines. To get the most for your remodeling dollars, you'll want to keep your projects in line with what other homes in your neighborhood have. If no one in your neighborhood has a pool, you'll probably recover even less than 46 percent of the cost. If most homes in your neighborhood have a fireplace, that addition to your house may get you more than 85 percent of the cost at the time you sell.

Insurance: Who Needs It? How Much? What Kind?

You must have some type of insurance. You can't legally drive a car without auto insurance. You absolutely should not be without some type of medical insurance. But life insurance does not necessarily fall into that category of must-have insurance.

Life insurance doesn't take care of you—when it comes time to collect, you're dead. It's designed to take care of your family. That's a simple concept, but one which many people forget, and so they spend too much on insurance that they don't need or buy the wrong type of insurance to take care of their needs.

Life Insurance for Singles without Dependents? Maybe Not.

If you are single and without dependents, you may not even need life insurance. However, if you've got a lot of debts, you may want a small policy to pay those debts and to cover funeral costs. You probably don't want to saddle relatives with those "final expenses," which is the euphemism insurance salespeople prefer.

Married, No Kids

If you are married but don't have any kids, you need to open the discussion with your spouse about how much he or she would need if you died and for how long the money would be needed. Let's say you are both employed, bring in fairly equal income, have similar expenses, and have incurred similar debt levels. If you died, your daily living costs—for clothes, transportation, food, and such—would be eliminated. Your spouse still would have to pay off the debts you've incurred. How much would it take to do that?

When it comes to rent or a mortgage, two people together can definitely cheaper than one person can. But your spouse might want to move to a smaller rental property or might want to sell the house and buy another home where the memories are not as fresh and constant.

The need for a hefty life insurance policy does exist if your spouse is still going to school or has little or no income. A disabled spouse or one who suffers from a medical condition that hinders employment may need a steady stream of money coming from an insurance policy.

Married with Children

Many insurance policies are sold on the assumption that your spouse and children will need a boatload of money. The spouse will then invest the money and your family will live off the earnings—and only the earnings—of that money. The boatload of money earning money—the principal—will never be touched.

Thus, if your contribution to the family income is $50,000, your spouse would need a life insurance policy that pays a sum of money that earns $50,000 a year. Work the problem backwards and assume that you get 10 percent after taxes on this hypothetical money. That means you would need a $500,000 life insurance policy. Factor inflation into the picture, and that $500,000 policy can get close to the $1 million mark.

You probably do need some type of life insurance if you are married with children, not only for the current expenses, but for future ones as well, such as college. You certainly want those "final expenses" paid, and it's a good idea to have enough insurance to pay off most of your debts—perhaps even your mortgage. Your spouse will be dealing first and foremost with the emotional devastation of your death. Life insurance can lift from your spouse the burden of worrying about making the payment on the auto loan or the mortgage.

Don't Forget the Primary Caregiver

Don't forget about an insurance policy on the spouse who is the primary caregiver for the children. This person may need as big a life insurance policy as the big breadwinner in the family.

If the primary caregiver dies, the survivor will have to pay an outside caregiver—and that person doesn't come cheap. That's an expense that won't go away until the children are into their teenage years. If your job takes you traveling a lot, you may even need a live-in caregiver for those teenaged children. You'll certainly need one for the children under the age of 14. Make sure a policy covers those expenses.

Assume Away

Whatever type of insurance you buy, make sure you are making the right assumptions. Don't let the salesman make them for you. The insurance salesman wants to sell you as much insurance as possible. You may not need it.

Many employers offer relatively inexpensive life insurance. The downside of employer-sponsored life insurance is that you leave it when you change jobs. Your new employer may not offer a life insurance benefit.

Take Social Security into Account

Social Security coughs up too. If you die, certain members of your family may be eligible for Social Security benefits. Rack up enough of the Social Security quarters—remember, 40 was the magic number—and the following family members can collect benefits:

- A surviving spouse of any age who is caring for a child under age 16.

- Your children, if they are unmarried and under the age of 18, or unmarried and under the age of 19 but still in elementary or secondary school full-time.

- A severely disabled child, whose disability must have started before he or she was 22 years old.

Social Security will pay your spouse and two children $1,801 dollars a month if you die at age 35, have the necessary quarterly credits and earned $40,000 in 1995. That won't get your family to Disney World, but it may cover the mortgage payment.

Approximate Monthly Survivors Benefits for Your Family If You Had Steady Earnings and Die in 1996

Your Age	Your Family		Your Earnings in 1996			
		$20,000	$30,000	$40,000	$50,000	$61,200 or more*
35	Your spouse and 1 child†	$1,179	$1,581	$1,801	$1,989	$2,150
	Your spouse and 2 children°	1,457	1,842	2,101	2,320	2,508
	1 child only	589	790	900	994	1,075
	Your spouse at age 60^	562	753	858	948	1,025
45	Your spouse and 1 child†	1,179	1,581	1,801	1,975	2,081
	Your spouse and 2 children°	1,457	1,842	2,101	2,303	2,427
	1 child only	589	790	900	987	1,040
	Your spouse at age 60^	562	753	858	941	992
55	Your spouse and 1 child†	1,179	1,579	1,766	1,878	1,946
	Your spouse and 2 children°	1,457	1,841	2,060	2,190	2,270
	1 child only	589	789	883	939	973
	Your spouse at age 60^	562	752	842	895	927

*Earnings equal or greater than the OASDI wage base from age 22 through 1995.

†Amounts shown also equal the benefits paid to two children, if no parent survives or surviving parent has substantial earnings.

°Equals the maximum family benefit.

^Amounts payable in 1996. Spouses turning 60 in the future would receive higher benefits.

Note: The accuracy of these three estimates depends on the pattern of your earnings in prior years.

Term Insurance

The most inexpensive and purest insurance, term life insurance policies, are often favored by young families with modest incomes but large insurance needs. A term policy covers a period of time—the term—for which you are insured. If you are 37-years-old, you might want a policy that covers you until you reach age 65. Thus, you would get a 28-year term policy.

You buy coverage in increments of $1,000. You pay the insurance company an annual premium, and they pay your beneficiary if you die. If you don't die by the end of the policy, the insurance company keeps all your premiums and wins the insurance bet. If you die before the term policy expires, your beneficiaries win the bet.

There are variations of term insurance. You can get a policy—called an annual renewable policy—in which the premiums rise year after year so that you pay less in your early years and more in your latter years for the same coverage. A policy in which the premium levels remain constant year after year also is available, but you will pay more in the early years for this policy than you would with an annual renewable policy.

You can also get term insurance that pays your beneficiaries a decreasing amount of money as you grow older. A twist to this decreasing term policy links your mortgage to your life insurance policy. The value of the policy decreases in line with the amount due on your mortgage.

You can attach a number of different bells and whistles—known as options or riders—to a term policy. You might consider the automatic right to renew the policy up to a certain age, no matter what happens to your health. Two other popular options are the right to convert your policy to whole life insurance and the "waiver of premium," which provides that your insurance will continue—with no further payments from you—if you are disabled.

You will probably want to pass on the double indemnity option which pays twice the amount in the case of death by accident or violence rather than disease. Dead is dead, as far as your family's financial situation goes. Their expenses are not going to double just because you died at the hands of a terrorist.

Whole Life Insurance

Also known as permanent life insurance, whole life insurance is more expensive than term because it covers you for your entire life as long as you pay the premiums. The premiums remain constant, although the younger you are when you first buy the insurance, the less you will pay each year. Still, you will be overpaying in your early years and underpaying in your later years.

Some of the value of your early-year payments goes into an account. If you cancel the policy before you die, you will collect that money. Let the money build up, and you can use it in your later years to pay your premium. You also may be able to borrow against it, and you don't need to repay the loan. Of course, the amount you borrowed will be deducted from the payment to your beneficiaries.

Like term insurance, whole life has its variations. A "limited payment life" policy lets you pay for a specific number of years, after which your policy is paid up. You make no additional payments, but your beneficiaries still will receive payment upon your death. An "endowment policy" lets you pay up early, and it also lets you collect the face value of your policy even if you are alive. These insurance policies are more expensive than term or regular whole life. Thus, if you buy policies with these features you may pay more for the same level of coverage or pay the same but have a lower level of benefits for your family.

Universal Life

Universal life insurance combines features of term and whole life insurance policies. You essentially buy term insurance but pay a little more than you might for a straight term policy. The difference you pay, though, goes into an investment account. The rate of return you earn on your money will vary, depending on how well the insurance company's investments perform, but you always are guaranteed a minimum rate. The money you earn does compound tax-deferred, like an IRA or 401(k).

You get flexibility with a universal life policy. You can change the death benefit, increase or decrease your premiums, and even borrow from the account. Take a look at how a universal policy works for William, who buys the policy at age 32.

Year Insured	William's Age	Annual Premium	Guaranteed Cash Value	Projected Value (8.5% Return)	Death Benefit
1	32	$1,200	$ 313	$ 313	$212,000
2	33	1,200	1,163	1,190	212,000
3	34	1,200	2,037	2,132	212,000
4	35	1,200	2,935	3,141	212,000
5	36	1,200	3,854	4,221	212,000
6	37	1,200	4,794	5,384	212,000
7	38	1,200	5,750	6,637	212,000
8	39	1,200	6,721	7,990	212,000
9	40	1,200	7,704	9,449	212,000
10	41	1,200	8,697	11,028	212,000
11	42	1,200	9,695	12,734	212,000
12	43	1,200	10,698	14,561	212,000
13	44	5,000	15,382	20,377	212,000
14	45	1,600	16,932	23,231	212,000
15	46	1,600	18,500	26,291	212,000
16	47	1,600	20,082	29,603	212,000
17	48	1,600	21,677	33,185	212,000
18	49	1,600	23,282	37,062	212,000
19	50	1,600	24,891	41,253	212,000
20	51	1,600	26,501	45,788	212,000
21	52	withdraws 5,000	21,345	43,641	207,000
22	53	withdraws 5,000	15,883	41,281	202,000
23	54	withdraws 5,000	10,090	38,694	197,000
24	55	withdraws 5,000	3,931	35,861	192,000
25	56	2,400	4,915	40,616	192,000
26	57	2,400	5,792	45,756	192,000
27	58	2,400	6,547	51,311	192,000
28	59	2,400	7,163	57,313	192,000
29	60	2,400	7,610	63,807	192,000
30	61	2,400	7,858	70,848	192,000
31	62	2,400	7,872	78,477	192,000
32	63	2,400	7,605	86,758	192,000
33	64	2,400	6,999	95,758	192,000
34	65	2,400	5,989	105,525	192,000
35	66	2,400	4,507	116,133	192,000

36	67	withdraws 20,000	policy	103,514	172,000
37	68	withdraws 20,000	canceled	89.809	152,000
38	69	withdraws 20,000		74,927	132,000
39	70	withdraws 20,000		58,761	112,000
40	71	withdraws 20,000		41,172	92,000
41	72	0		43,689	92,000
42	73	0		46,333	92,000
43	74	0		49,132	92,000
44	75	0		52,117	92,000

Universal life insurance also comes in a shape that makes it look like an IRA or 401(k). Universal variable life insurance allows you to decide how your money will be invested. Every insurance company takes a profit and charges you for administering the policy. To compare variable universal life policies, ask different insurance firms to give you the "projected cash buildup" of the policy. Make sure you use the same interest rate for comparisons.

The projected cash buildup represents the investment portion—which is separate from the specified death benefit dollars—of the policy. If the death benefit is the same on both policies, you then compare the projected cash buildup. Generally, the policy with the higher buildup will be better because it indicates that the insurance firm is taking a smaller fee for managing the account. That way, you can determine how much the firm is charging for administrative costs and how much it's taking out in the form of profits.

Invest It Yourself or Use Insurance as an Investment Vehicle?

As you can see, there are many different kinds of insurance, and many policies have dual personalities in that they have investment aspects attached to them. Try to stay focused on what the policy does for your family if you die rather than on the investment portion of the policy. You have other options for retirement investments such as IRAs and 401(k)s, which may work better for you. Carefully evaluate any insurance policy that sports an investment feature—and they all do except for straight term insurance. Ask yourself:

- What's the difference in cost between straight term and this other policy?

- How much interest will my money earn with the insurance policy?

- Could I invest the difference in cost between straight term and this policy?

- What would that difference earn me in a tax-deferred account?

You may find you are better off investing the difference in an IRA or 401(k). What's the advantage of buying an investmentlike insurance plan that offers an investment opportunity rather than sticking with a straight IRA or 401(k) plan? There isn't any major financial advantage. But there may be a practical advantage for you.

Many financial experts advise, "Buy term insurance and invest the difference." That's a good strategy as long as you do invest the difference. If you don't or won't, you should consider an insurance policy that has investment features to be sure you're taking care of your investment needs for retirement.

Annuities: IRAs without the Investment Limits

Annuities act like IRAs, but they allow you to contribute more than the IRA investment ceiling imposed on individuals and couples. Created by insurance companies to offer the same tax advantages as IRAs, annuities have become very popular, particularly among people 50 years and older.

You can buy an annuity with a lump sum, or you can spread your payments over time. Annuities come in two basic flavors—fixed and variable—but also offer lots of different sprinkles and toppings.

Fixed-Rate and Variable Annuities

Here's how a fixed annuity works. You give the insurance company your money, and the company invests it however it likes. The insurance company guarantees to pay you a fixed rate of return. It doesn't matter to you how well or how poorly the insurance company invests that money: They have to pay you that guaranteed rate. Just make sure you go with a reputable company that isn't likely to go belly-up.

With a variable rate annuity, you tell the insurance company how you want your money invested from among a number of offerings such as stock, bond, and money market accounts. Like an IRA and a 401(k), you can switch from fund to fund without paying taxes. The smarter you are at investing, the more money you'll reap.

Annuity Payments

You can't get those payments for a number of years, and most annuities are designed to begin paying you when you reach retirement age. You do have a choice concerning how you'll withdraw the funds. You can get funds until you die, until you and your spouse die, or for a specific number of years, in which case your spouse gets the annuity benefits if you die before that specified period of time.

One of the most popular choices is to get a specific amount of money every month until you die. This cuts the risk that you'll outlive your investments.

You Assemble the Pieces

You've got lots of options for your investments and for the plans or accounts in which you put those investments. Think of your home as a possible investment plan. Ditto for insurance.

Of course, some options are better than others, and some will work better for you than for someone else. There's no hard rule for which pieces go into your retirement program. Knowing your options and the advantages and drawbacks of those options gives you the freedom to write your own retirement screenplay and direct the movie you envision.

Like the director who interviews writers, actors, and set designers, you also will be reviewing bankers, insurance brokers, mutual funds, and the like to find which ones will make your retirement flick an award-winning one. Chapter nine will introduce you to the folks who you will be directing.

A CAST of thousands working FOR YOU

CHAPTER NINE

*You've got the vision for your retirement plan. Now you'll need a cast and crew to bring your retirement **vision** to the silver screen. There are tens of thousands of **people** in Investment Land who are willing, anxious, and, in some cases, downright desperate to be a part of your retirement production.*

You've got the vision for your retirement plan. Now you'll need a cast and crew to help you carry it off. There are tens of thousands of people who are willing, anxious, and, in some cases, downright desperate to be a part of your retirement plan. Some are more skilled than others. Some are better at one task than another. With so many willing helpers, you can be selective in whom you choose.

You Hold the Power, You Hold the Purse Strings

Banks, securities firms, insurance companies, and mutual fund companies are all competing for the chance to help you with your retirement plan. Be selective and demand service. You are the one holding the power in the relationship. You are the one with the money—whether it's $2,000 or $20,000—and they want that money to open a plan or account for you or to invest it for you.

Moreover, you are not bound to stay with any insurance firm, bank, brokerage firm, or mutual fund just because you bought an IRA or an insurance contract from them. If any member of your crew is not meeting your standards, you can find someone else to do the job. Be careful, though, not to let your anger lead you into a misstep. Don't rush to pull out funds, close an account, or cancel a policy until you know where you are going next. A hasty decision could create immediate tax penalties and future tax problems.

WHO'S A FINANCIAL ADVISER AND WHO'S NOT?

Insurance agents, stockbrokers, and bankers all like to call themselves **financial advisers.** They may understand financial planning. Then again, maybe they just want to sell you a product. There is a professional organization that certifies financial planners in much the same way that accountants get the certified public account designation.

Look for the **Certified Financial Planner (CFP)** initials after your adviser's name. That means your agent has gotten the seal of approval—and taken courses and passed exams along the way—from the Institute of Certified Financial Planners.

Long Ago and Far Away

There was a time when the jobs these financial institutions did and the products they sold were very distinct from one another. Bankers handled checking and savings accounts and gave out loans. Savings and loans provided savings accounts and offered mortgages. Securities firms bought and sold stocks and bonds. Mutual fund companies sold mutual funds.

Each industry was regulated by a separate U.S. government entity. Banks could not sell insurance.

Brokerage firms could not offer checking-account-like products and insurance firms could not sell mutual funds.

In the mid-1970s things began to change. Securities brokerage firms started getting into the lending business by offering to individuals cash management accounts—glorified but limited savings accounts—from which you could take out short-term loans. Insurance firms started offering investments that looked a lot like the products peddled by the brokerage firms. The banks searched for loopholes to allow them to sell stocks and bonds.

Since then, the lines separating these different kinds of companies have become blurred. After years of playing catch-up, the federal government has been responding to this new investment world. So what does this mean for you?

Today, the rules surrounding selling insurance are pretty much the same whether the sales company is an insurance firm or a bank. Ditto for mutual funds and IRAs. That's good news for you because it means that everybody courting you to buy a mutual fund or insurance policy has to play by the same rules. They may be regulated by different Washington agencies, but the regulations enforced by the bureaucrats are pretty much the same.

Some Create, Some Sell, and Some Do Both

With the lines blurred, there is another way to look at the people so eager to set up retirement plans for you and invest your money—in short, to sell you something. Most of the players create and sell investment products. Understanding who does what will provide a framework for you to assess the various products and services—and the motivations of those who offer them to you.

Often, those who create the products they sell directly to you can offer the products cheaper or at the same price but with more services. Buying directly from the creator can cut administrative fees, too.

It's like buying generic brands at the supermarket or a designer T-shirt at the manufacturer's outlet. Buy direct, and you cut out the middleman. Of course, the outlet store probably won't supply you with a gift box and tissue whereas a department store will.

In the the investment world, the seller who creates often sells you the product at the same price that everyone else does, but also offers more services. When it comes to investments, you must decide if you need those services enough to pay extra for them.

IT'S A COUPLE THING

Make sure you and your spouse **involve each other** when you shape your retirement plan. Here are some tips for couples.

• **Agree** on whatever decision you are going to take.

• **Appoint** one record keeper.

• **Meet together** with your helpers. That way you can be sure you are both getting the same information.

• Try not to undermine your spouse by criticizing or demeaning your partner in front of a provider. It creates an opportunity for the representative to play the divide-and-conquer game, not unlike the one your kids play when they get the chance.

Insurance Firms

Insurance firms write insurance policies. Many sell them directly through sales forces they employ. Independent insurance agents might sell policies from a number of different companies. Banks, too, can sell insurance. So can securities brokerage firms.

Insurance salespeople often suggest meeting face-to-face with you to discuss "your investment needs." Go ahead and meet, get the information, but don't make a snap decision. Read over the literature and think about what is being offered, where else you might get a similar product, and at what cost.

Insurance salespeople are famous for their enthusiasm about insurance. They will tell you that there's an insurance policy to meet every investment need you have. That's true. But that policy may not *best* meet the investment needs you have. Remember the advice: "Buy term insurance and invest the difference." You also may want to investigate annuity products.

Securities Firms

Securities firms help to create stocks and bonds, which are the building blocks of mutual funds. They also create mutual funds, which they sell directly. They may sell them to banks, which slap their own brand name on them and then resell them to you. The mutual fund itself doesn't change even though it has a new name. The bank, as a middleman, may take a "cut" in the form of a fee it charges to you.

Securities firms employ small armies of people who call themselves stockbrokers. These people don't actually go to the floor of the New York Stock Exchange and buy and sell stocks and bonds for you. They are salespeople who make their money selling investments to you. They may call themselves financial advisers, but they are really salespeople. The best, though, want to keep your business and will therefore offer you retirement planning advice.

Mutual Funds

Mutual fund companies create mutual funds. These may be rebranded and sold through a securities firm or a bank or an insurance company. Most mutual fund companies either sell through a third party or sell directly to you via the mail or the electronic highways.

Mutual funds make it relatively easy for you to bypass the middleman and invest directly with big firms. You fill out the appropriate forms and then just send them money or have your bank or securities firm transfer money from your account. You tell the mutual fund company how you want your money invested. You get regular statements and often can call on the phone, punch a few buttons, and review the status of your account.

When you call with questions, you normally won't deal with the same person. That may not be a problem because the mutual funds tend to spend a lot of money training their employees about the investments they offer and what those investments do. They don't spend a lot of money training a slew of people to *sell* you mutual funds, since they have the securities firms, insurance companies, and banks out there to do that for them.

Banks

Banks can create their own mutual funds and their own insurance policies, or they can merely peddle someone else's. If you're buying into a mutual fund through a bank, ask who created the mutual fund. Sometimes banks will sell you a mutual fund, but another firm manages the fund and a third firm might handle the paperwork and customer complaints. This is not a problem as long as you have the information about where to lodge a complaint.

You may feel most comfortable opening an IRA with the bank with which you normally transact business. Your bank can be a good place to start if you feel nervous just thinking about dealing with a mutual fund or securities firm to open an IRA, for instance.

In the past, federal regulators were particularly strict about letting banks get into any business other than banking. Now that restrictions have been eliminated, the banks are playing catch-up. Many are being very aggressive and innovative in the investment products they offer and the prices at which they are selling these products. Other banks, though, play a me-too game with also-ran results. Do comparison shopping among banks and the other players when it comes to retirement accounts and investments.

HIT THE ROAD, JACK

Run like the wind if a salesperson:

• **Scares** you. Anybody who frightens you is even scarier handling your retirement program.

• Makes you feel **dumb.**

• Wants you to make an **immediate decision.**

• Makes you feel **uncomfortable.**

Settle for the Best

With so many competing for the chance to help you make your retirement plan an award-winning one, you can and should demand a high level of service. You also want the most competent folks working for you.

Don't let inferior institutions and people waste your time and money. There are a number of things you can do to get good support. Look for people who are willing to give you information up front and can clearly explain how investments work. It's that person's job to communicate to you, and if you don't understand, it is that person's fault, not yours. Understanding investments is really not rocket-scientist material. If you're finding yourself confused even after a representative has attempted an explanation, it may very well be that the rep doesn't understand it either.

What to Ask

Here are some questions to ask and areas to cover when you're looking for an adviser:

- What federal and state agencies regulate this investment and where do people lodge complaints?

- Ask for the name and address of the head of the company. Tell the adviser that you intend to let that person know when you're happy with the products you buy and the services you get—and that you'll be communicating your displeasure, as well. Don't be timid about following through.

- Ask how many clients the salesperson handles. Beware of salespeople who tell you they have 2,500 clients and all their clients get personalized service. Think about it. There are only about 250 working days in every year. If your salesperson works 10 hours a day, that's 2,500 working hours a year for 2,500 clients. Do you think that one hour a year constitutes personalized service?

- Ask the salespeople how they make their money. Are they paid a salary, or do they make their money from a commission fee based on what they sell you? There is no right or wrong answer, but you have a right to know what is the self-interest of the salesperson in selling you an investment product.

- Don't feel compelled to buy an investment just because you attended a free seminar and got a little box lunch or even a rubber chicken dinner.

- Ask for a list of clients—at least a half dozen. Make sure the list contains

Fraud Busters

Beware of schemes that could scuttle your dreams.

The golden rule for avoiding investment scams long has been, "If it sounds too good to be true, it probably is." Still, Americans get stung for millions of dollars every year by con artists offering fraudulent investment deals. Here are some of the most common scams being perpetrated in the 1990s and some tips on how to avoid them.

Penny Stocks: Penny stocks are inexpensive stocks usually issued for new business ventures. At their best, legitimate penny stocks are extremely speculative; at their worst, their prices are easily manipulated by the company issuing the stock and by unscrupulous broker–dealers. Too often, unsuspecting investors get stuck with worthless paper certificates entitling them to 1,000 shares of a company that is tumbling into bankruptcy.

Precious Metals: Gold jewelry glitters, but be leery about some gold investments. Typically, investors are persuaded to invest in gold, silver, or platinum with promises of skyrocketing prices. The reality is that many of these investments are very illiquid, highly speculative, or merely phony.

Real Estate: The most common real estate scams involve fraudulent real estate tax shelters, multiple sales of the same worthless land, and developments whose values have been artificially inflated. Overselling or misrepresenting time-share units is another popular rip-off.

Ponzi Schemes: One of the oldest scams is the Ponzi scheme, which works on the principle of hundreds of Peters paying a few Pauls. Also known as pyramid schemes, early investors—in commodities, real estate, or gold mines, you name it—are paid off or rewarded with money coming from succeeding waves of investors, who must lure even more investors into the pyramid so they can get paid off. Eventually, the last investors lose the most and the promoters walk away rich—unless the authorities nab them. The scheme gets its name from Charles A. Ponzi, who ran just such a scam on a huge scale during the 1920s.

Oil & Gas: While a very legitimate investment, oil and gas properties have also been used by con artists. Rip-off schemes involve using false drilling equipment placed on worthless land. Some scams promise huge new "discoveries" of oil in an area where there are no known petroleum deposits.

You can steer clear of getting taken by following a few simple rules:

- Never invest over the telephone.

- Be highly suspicious of any scheme which requires your "immediate" investment.

- Check out the company with the Better Business Bureau, your state securities office, and the Securities and Exchange Commission.

- Be wary of outrageous promises like 60 percent interest rates or 50-to-1 returns on real estate or a 500 percent annual profit.

A steady and diversified approach to retirement investing is a much surer path to your long-term financial security than get-rich-quick schemes that only let others get rich while you are left holding a bag of nothing.

people who are in similar circumstances as you are. The client with $5 million in investments is not a good reference point for you if you're investing a few thousand. If your agent has no clients with profiles similar to yours, you might consider looking elsewhere.

What to Watch for After You're on Board

- Expect your calls to be returned promptly.

- Lodge a complaint if you're being shuttled from one person to the next. If your securities broker sells you an IRA and investments for that IRA, you shouldn't have to deal with other people.

- The red warning light should go on if a salesperson is constantly calling you with "great investments." The salesperson should understand that the investments in your retirement plan are for the long term and therefore do not need to be frequently changed. Moreover, the salesperson's focus on "great investments" suggests a lack of understanding about your retirement plan which concerns good asset allocation and diversification, not just individual great investments.

- Sirens should go off if your salesperson forever wants you to switch from one investment to another. This is a good indicator that he's probably just trying to make a commission. Your retirement savings are for the long term. You'll want to switch some money from one investment to another so your asset allocation fits your circumstances. But that doesn't mean moving from one mutual fund to another every six months or a year.

If you're doing business with a stockbroker at a large securities firm, ask the broker if there are any seminars available about investments or retirement planning. Suggest that, with your busy schedule, a lunch or dinner seminar would work best for you. You'll probably get invited—and to more than just one meal.

Dissatisfied and Ready to Change?

Are you put on permanent hold every time you call? Are your investments decreasing while the fees just keep going up? If you're dissatisfied with your bank or securities firm, here's what you do:

- Voice your concerns to the person who is your contact at the company— probably the person who sold you in the first place. Don't shout. Be polite. If you are still dissatisfied . . .

- Ask what can be done to change the picture and if there will be any added costs or consequences to making such a change. For example, find out if you can get better service for an additional fee or if you would get a better rate of return by switching investments, which, in turn, would require paying a "switching fee" plus a commission.

- Start looking at alternatives. What are other banks, mutual funds, or brokerage firms offering? How does it compare with what you're getting?

- Write a letter to the head of the department or even the head of the company. Outline your concerns and ask how things might be changed for the better. You can offer some suggestions based on your research.

- Talk to some of those alternatives. Explain that you are considering moving your account and ask how they could help you do that so that you don't risk any tax consequences. Line up at least two new companies.

- Let your representative at the original company know you intend to transfer your account. At this time, you may discover all kinds of enticements thrown your way to keep you. If you are upset about fees or paperwork, you may find the institution is willing to cut them or meet your request. If the problem is with the returns you're getting—significantly lower than comparable returns elsewhere—you might want to pass up those enticements. The key to growing your investments is boosting your returns, not cutting your fees.

Let the Three Amigos Help You Direct Your Helpers

The three amigos—asset allocation, diversification, and leverage—also can be employed to help you manage your retirement plan, crew, and cast. Allocate your business to those institutions that do the best job for a specific investment plan or investment. Diversify your business among different players. This gives you two advantages: you get to compare performance, and you spread your risk.

Leveraging means making your cast work as hard for you as you are doing for your employer. Your agents should be supplying you with information about your investments, any changes in the tax code that might impact those investments, timely records, and regular statements. Get these people to do as much as possible (for free, of course). You're in charge. Review the information and ask the strategic questions. If you act with authority, you'll be treated with respect.

FINE-tune your retirement PLAN

CHAPTER TEN

The difference between an Oscar-contender and an Oscar-winning film lies in the details and fine-tuning. So it goes with your retirement plan. A **snip** *here, a change there can create a retirement plan that will age as well as* **you do.**

With your three amigos helping you, your retirement investments can grow with very little work on your part. But don't be a total couch potato. Every couple of years you should tally your total retirement investments and calculate the percentage you have amassed in each investment category—bonds, growth and income stocks, and aggressive growth stocks, for example. You may be surprised at what you find.

Let's say you originally decided to allocate your contributions to your retirement plan using the "100 minus age equal equities" formula. Three years ago, at age 25, that formula called for at least 75 percent of your investments to be placed in equities. Being gutsy and young, you put 80 percent into equities and only 20 percent into bonds. Originally your asset allocation looked like this:

Bond fund	20%
Growth and income stock fund	40%
Aggressive growth stock fund	40%
Total	100%

After three years, you notice that your retirement investments total $10,000 and look like this:

Bond fund	$500	equals 5% of your investments
Growth & income stock fund	3,000	equals 30% of your investments
Aggressive growth stock fund	6,500	equals 65% of your investments
Total	10,000	equals 100% of your investments

What happened? Why do your investments no longer reflect your original 20 percent/40 percent/40 percent asset allocation?

What happened is that the money you invested in the aggressive growth fund grew much faster than the money you invested in the growth and income mutual stock funds and in the bond fund.

Reconfigure Your Investment Portfolio

To put your portfolio back on the original 20 percent/40 percent/40 percent path you set for it, you need to reconfigure your asset allocation. Doing that will probably be easier than programming your VCR.

Why bother? With the aggressive growth stocks doing so spectacularly well, why not keep 65 percent of your investments in that fast-growing fund? Your amigo diversification says, "No way." Your retirement investments would be subject to too much risk if your aggressive growth stock fund should decline 40 percent over a couple of months and then reside in those lower levels while other aggressive growth funds spiral higher.

To reduce that risk and maintain your friendship with diversification, you'll want to transfer money out of the aggressive growth fund and into the bond fund and the growth and income stock funds. Your portfolio then would look like this:

Bond fund	$ 2,000	equals 20% of your investments
Growth & income stock fund	4,000	equals 40% of your investments
Aggressive growth stock fund	4,000	equals 40% of your investments
Total	10,000	equals 100% of your investments

Reconfiguring is easy. You may need to complete some paperwork for your plan administrator and place your signature on some dotted lines. The small amount of time you allocate to this task can create some solid financial resources for your retirement.

How unbalanced should your portfolio be before you reconfigure? Generally, you should assess your situation every five to ten years. If you are off by 10% or more, then you need to take action.

Once you realize how incredibly easy it is to reconfigure, you may be tempted to fiddle with your investments every few months or even from week to week. Resist the urge. Let your investments grow a couple of years before your next reconfiguration.

Of course, you will want to reallocate your entire portfolio every five years with the "100 minus age equals equities" formula. In the meantime, though, you can relax.

The Rating Game

Rating the performance of over 7,500 mutual funds has gained Olympic-sport status in the investment world. Magazines, newspapers, and professional journals herald their own rankings with the fanfare and self-congratulatory remarks of newscasters announcing the achievements of the home-grown team. With so many published lists, it's hard to find a mutual fund that does not achieve top status on at least one.

How then can you sift the good from the bad, the solid from the mediocre among so many investment choices? Look at the rankings of the three major rating services.

These services employ battalions of analysts to research the performance of mutual funds. Leverage your research efforts by letting them do the grunt work for you. You can subscribe to the services or you can get the information free at the library. See the resources section of this book for contact information.

Morningstar dispenses one to five stars to the 4,442 mutual funds it rates. For $395 a year, *Morningstar* will give you all these ratings, provide updates every two weeks, and supply you with detailed information about each of the mutual funds it rates.

The Value Line Investment Survey uses a one-to-five rating system for the 4,145 mutual funds it covers. (One is the highest rating.) The price is $295 a year.

Lipper Analytical Services grades a whopping 4,300 mutual funds and provides detailed information on 3,500 of them. Some 150 newspapers carry the ratings. You can get the more detailed information by subscribing to Lipper.

You could save yourself these subscription fees by visiting your library. Most major ones subscribe to at least one, if not all, of these rating services. But don't just rely on the ratings. Examine the information these services provide on each individual mutual fund.

Snipping and Shaving Fees

The world of investing is littered with fees. You pay a fee to a bank, for instance, to be the custodian of your IRA. You may pay a fee to a brokerage house to buy the growth and income stock fund you have purchased to put into your IRA. And then, you will pay—though the fee is somewhat buried—the mutual fund to manage the money within that fund.

Look what happens to your investment returns when you factor in a $25 fee here and a $25 fee there. Let's say you have $5,000 of retirement investments that earn 10 percent or $500 in a tax-deferred account. Those total fees of $50 cut your annual return from 10 percent to 9.5 percent.

The more money you have in your account, the smaller the impact will be on the rate of return. Still, it's a good idea to keep close watch on the various fees attached to your retirement investments. There are some tactics for keeping those fees to a minimum.

Do comparative shopping. If your bank or brokerage firm is charging you significantly more, for instance, as custodian of your IRA, than most others are charging, bring the disparity to the attention of a supervisor. Ask for your fees to be reduced. If you are a long-time customer but are given the brush-off, you might start shopping for a new IRA custodian.

Many funds waive some or a portion of some fees if the value of your account reaches a certain level. But stock and bonds markets go down as well as up. Sometimes, a market decline will push the value of your investments below the freebie fee level. Should that happen, ask if your fee might be waived for a year.

You can also try to jettison a fee charged by a mutual fund if your mutual fund significantly underperforms the market. Let's say you invest in a growth and income mutual fund. The fund declines 15 percent one year and another 10 percent the next. Meanwhile, according to the rating services, growth and income funds averaged a 20 percent increase one year and a 17 percent rise the next. Such a lackluster performance hardly needs to be rewarded. Approach a representative of the mutual fund and suggest a waiver on whatever fees you can negotiate.

Pulling the Plug

As smart as you are and as diligent as you have been in picking good investments, you may find that you occasionally pick a dog. No need to focus on mistakes. With a diversified portfolio of investments and with time on your side, a bowwow investment will not take a huge bite from the total you might expect to amass in 25 to 30 years.

Knowing when and why it's time to sell is as important as understanding what you want to buy. Your sell signals, though, are not linked to what is happening in the stock or bond markets. There are a number of reasons for selling an investment within your overall retirement plan.

The individual investment just may not be performing well. You must distinguish, though, between a subpar performance by your specific investment and a subpar performance by investments in that category.

For instance, most people under age 40 should have some portion of their retirement investments in aggressive growth stocks. But what if your aggressive growth mutual fund has consistently underperformed most other aggressive growth funds? You notice the three rating services give your fund low marks. You read the detailed information the services have gathered about your fund and discover few good things are being said about the aggressive growth fund you have picked. Well, it's probably time to sell that fund and buy another aggressive growth fund.

Another reason for selling a stock is to reconfigure your portfolio or to bring your asset allocation into line with your age. The asset allocation formula tells you which category of investments to buy and which ones to sell.

Don't be too hasty to sell an underperforming investment. Research why the stock, bond, or mutual fund has been crawling among the nether regions. It's time to sell once you are satisfied that you could do a lot better with a number of different investments within the same category.

Know the Risks So You Can Take Them

There is no such thing as a risk-free investment. Even dollars stuffed into a strongbox carry a risk because inflation will make those greenbacks worth less tomorrow than they are today.

While you may enjoy white-water rafting and skiing in the powder, when it comes to investing, you may be rather risk-adverse. You associate taking risk with losing money. But in the world of investing, taking risk is the key to getting bigger returns which make your investments work harder for you.

One of the biggest mistakes you can make is to sink all your money into ultraconservative investments which bring you low rate of returns. The reason is that these investments barely keep pace with inflation. To get your investments growing strong, you need to outpace inflation by more than a point or two.

To construct a framework for your long-term investing goals, you need to understand the various types of risk associated with investments. Once you understand those basic risks, you can examine your specific situation to determine how much of what type of risk you feel comfortable assuming.

The younger you are, the more risk you can assume. That's because younger folk have a longer time period to recoup low or negative returns from higher risk investments. These higher risk investments generally produce higher returns if they are held over the long term. Take a look at the different types of risks various investments face.

Inflation Risk

This is the certainty that even the smallest bit of inflation will erode the purchasing power of your money over the long term. One way to lessen this risk is to invest your money with the goal of earning a rate of return which is at least a couple of points above the inflation rate.

Interest Rate Risk

As inflation rises, so do interest rates. And as interest rates rise, the value of some investments—bonds, for example—fall. The returns you get on other investments, such as some stocks, may move counter to interest rates and bonds, although most will fill with rising rates. Cash investments like CDs and money market funds tend to benefit from higher interest rates. One way to lessen this risk is to make sure you allocate your assets so that all your investments are not closely linked to interest rate moves.

Business Risk

This is the specific risk associated with the underlying institution represented by the stock, bond, or other investment. For instance, if someone discovered a $5 cure for every ailment that afflicts the human race, the pharmaceutical industry would probably go the way of the buggy-whip industry. As far-fetched as that may seem, small events can impact mightily on the fortunes of individual companies and whole industries. Moreover, every company and every industry faces certain business risks from advances in technology, huge class-action lawsuits, and unwise business decisions. Diversifying your investments can help reduce this type of risk.

Market Risk

This is the risk that the entire equities or debt markets will plummet. This happened in the equities markets in October 1987 and again in October 1989. The bond market collapsed in October 1979 and in February 1995. But over the long run, these markets regained their losses and moved even higher.

The best way to reduce market risk is to invest consistently and steadily. That way, you take advantage of market declines thanks to dollar-cost-averaging, which lets you buy more shares when markets decline than you could buy when they are going higher.

Trying to guess the direction of the stock and bond markets and then buying according to that guess is called market timing, and it's not only a waste of your time, but it is counterproductive to growing your investments. That's because in order for market timing to work, you must correctly identify each market high and low. Miss only a couple and your investments will be worth less—over the long term—than with a steady, consistent investing plan in both up markets and down markets.

Currency Risk

Currency fluctuations affect the value of your investments in foreign countries and of your investments in U.S. companies that do business abroad. Prices can whipsaw as a result of currency devaluations, limitations imposed on the amount of money that can be taken out of a foreign country, and general and wide-scale political upheavals. Diversification helps cut the risk.

Spread the Risks

Most investments carry more than one type of risk. Equities carry market risk, but they also can be impacted by interest rates, though less than bonds.

The important thing to remember is that risk is linked to reward. Higher risk produces higher returns over the long term. Allocate and then diversify, and you will eliminate a lot of unnecessary risk from your investment plan.

Shots for the Singles

Nearly 30 percent of the American population is single. If you're in that group, you'll want to tailor your retirement plan to meet your needs. Here are a few issues for a single person to keep in mind.

Financial Education

In marriage, it's typical—though not necessarily advisable—that one person handles the heavy-duty finances like investing and buying insurance. As a single person, it's absolutely essential that you learn the basics of retirement planning.

Budgeting

Clothing, entertainment, and credit cards can drain the paycheck of young singles when retirement seems so far away. Yet, you need to start saving for a home and investing for retirement. Many suddenly single parents need to budget just to make ends meet. It may mean moving to a smaller house and not overindulging the children so that money can be spent on necessities. One of those necessities is retirement planning. Remember to take care of yourself first so you can then take care of your children.

Disability Insurance

Without a partner to share financial responsibilities, a single person unable to work because of a disability can quickly get into financial trouble. So, consider purchasing disability insurance which replaces a portion of lost wages. Your employer and Social Security may provide some benefits, but you may need more or better coverage.

Health Insurance

Buy it if you are not adequately covered through work. If you are between jobs, try to continue coverage under your old employer or purchase short-term health insurance. If you are divorced with children, see if your ex-spouse's insurance will cover the children.

Life Insurance

Not all singles need life insurance. But, if you have children, it's essential. An ex-spouse providing child support should be covered, too. Minors can't collect insurance proceeds, so your will should establish a trust beneficiary so the money can be managed for their benefit until they reach the age of 18 or 21.

NOW, back to the FUTURE

CHAPTER ELEVEN

To calculate where you are going, you need to know what you spend now and what your current income and invest-ments are. We supply the calculating charts that turn current dollars into **future dollars** *and take into account inflation and the rates of* **return** *on your investments.*

Now that you know how to create your own retirement plan, it's time to start figuring how much you need to save today for a comfortable retirement many tomorrows hence. It's not difficult, but it does take some computing. So rev up your calculator, and let's go.

The more accurate the information you plug into the equations, the more effective your results will be. But if the information is not readily available, it's better to estimate than to leave out the information altogether. You can always fine-tune the numbers later.

Keep these forms handy. You'll want to update the numbers to take into account changes in your employment, your family situation, and the investments you will be making for your retirement.

And, you probably will want to keep track of your progress as you build your retirement program. A steady and consistent plan will give you the retirement life you want.

Calculate Your Income and Your Expenses

To calculate where you are going, you need to know what you spend now and what your current income and investments are. The following charts help you make the calculations that turn current dollars into future dollars.

Remember to use current dollars. Don't worry about inflation factors and rates of returns on your investments. The charts take all that into consideration.

Expenses Now and in Retirement

The standard rule of thumb says your annual retirement income will need to equal between 70 percent and 80 percent of your current annual income in order for you to maintain your current lifestyle. There are a variety of reasons that you will need less in retirement than you do now.

Your taxes will be less because you will be earning less. You also won't be working, so you may be able to totally avoid paying Social Security tax. If your income is particularly robust in retirement, you will have to pay Social Security something, but not as much as you are now paying.

You'll be spending less money on your kids, who will presumably be taking care of themselves. You also will have acquired life's big-ticket items—appliances, furniture, and the like—and although you may have to replace some of these from time to time, these big expenses should be minimized. You'll be spending less money for clothes and dry cleaning because you won't be working full-time.

Moreover, you'll have more time to shop wisely. And you will be able to take advantage of all those discount and half-price offers available to seniors for everything from movie tickets to airline seats to motel rooms.

Here are some estimates of what you can expect your retirement expenses to be.

- *Housing*. Your housing costs should decline by 25 percent to 30 percent if you pay off your mortgage by retirement and have maintained your house and property. If you plan to sell your home and buy a smaller one, this housing expense will decrease even further. Don't forget, though, to add in that monthly fee if you plan to move into a condominium. And remember, you'll still be paying property taxes.

- *Utilities*. These will probably be pretty much the same unless you plan to spend most of your retirement time in your home, in which case you might add a little to the utility costs. Of course, if your kids are running up the utility bills with electronic gadgetry and 30-minute showers twice a day, your current bill may be more than your retirement bill will be.

- *Household services*. Subtract any child-care costs, but add costs for maintaining the yard and shoveling snow if you plan to live in a cold climate. You probably won't want to take on these tasks in your retirement years.

- *Maintenance*. You'll still need to get the gutters cleaned, the fence fixed, and the water boiler replaced when it goes kaput.

- *Clothing*. Your clothing costs may decline by 20 percent to 35 percent when you move from workplace clothes to jeans or slacks. You probably will be spending less money on dry cleaning, too.

- *Food*. Your food costs actually may be more because you may want to eat out more often. If you love your own cooking, you may find your food costs will be less.

- *Transportation*. While you can eliminate your current commuting cost, you might add the cost of more day-tripping and auto travel. Maintaining your car costs the same.

- *Gifts.* Whether it takes the form of donations to charitable, political, or religious organizations or presents to family members and friends, the amount of money you spend on gifts will not change in retirement. While you will no longer be contributing to the United Way or to the community halfway house through your workplace, the number of members of your family may increase as your children have children.

- *Education.* Scratch this. You won't be putting the kids through college or saving for such, unless you intend to fund your grandchildren's education. If you plan to take some courses, remember that tuition breaks are available to seniors.

- *Insurance* (life, property, auto, and liability). These insurance costs will remain the same. The one exception is life insurance, which you may wish to reduce if the rest of your retirement program is firmly in place. You may be able to reduce your life insurance cost by 50 percent.

- *Medical and dental insurance and expenses.* Premiums, deductibles, and out-of-pocket costs will rise by about 50 percent.

- *Loans.* Plan to be free of debt by the time you retire. And put a big ZERO in the "retirement" column.

- *Personal care and health clubs.* Probably about the same unless you expect to hire your own personal trainer (add more) or become a vegetating ancient (subtract some). Some people find they have more time for these pursuits when they retire. If you haven't been exercising due to a lack of time and you start after retirement, the cost may increase.

- *Entertainment.* This includes hobbies, videocassettes, sports events, concerts, vacations, and travel. You can take advantage of senior discounts for some of these expenses, but you'll be spending more money overall. Add about 20 percent to what you currently spend.

- *Savings and retirement.* Okay, you are not going to be contributing at the current level, but financial experts suggest that retired people continue to save about 10 percent of their income. The more you save now, the less you may need to contribute to this category during retirement. It's your choice.

- *Taxes.* You may not have to pay any Social Security taxes in retirement if you are below a certain income level. Under current laws, the most you may have to pay on is 85 percent of your FICA benefits. But don't forget about the taxes you will have to pay on the income as you begin to withdraw money from your IRA or pension plan.

- *Relatives.* This means your children and grandchildren. Remember, the example you set for them today will help them learn to take care of themselves tomorrow. That way, you won't have to help support them in the future. You will have less leeway when it comes to your parents if they have not done a good job of their retirement planning. But you can be a model for them, too. Talk to your parents about what you're planning for your retirement—it's not too late for them to start.

Use this chart to get a good handle on your current expenses and to estimate what your retirement expenses will be. (If this exercise seems too difficult, just take your total income before taxes, multiply it by 0.8 and skip to the next chart. Working your way through the whole thing, however, will give you a better, more accurate prediction of what your expenses might be.)

Expense	Current Cost	Retirement Cost
Housing	_____	_____
Utilities	_____	_____
Household Services	_____	_____
Maintenance	_____	_____
Clothing	_____	_____
Food	_____	_____
Transportation	_____	_____

Gifts	_____	_____
Education	_____	_____
Insurance	_____	_____
Medical and Dental	_____	_____
Loans	_____	_____
Personal Care/Health Clubs	_____	_____
Entertainment	_____	_____
Savings/Retirement	_____	_____
Taxes	_____	_____
Relatives	_____	_____
TOTAL	_____	_____

Your total current expenses should be equal to your total pretax income. Now divide your expected retirement expenses by your total current expenses/income. That will give you the percentage of your current income you will need in retirement.

If your estimate is less than 70 percent of your current income, you may be setting yourself up for a bare-bones retirement. If it's more than 80 percent, you probably are anticipating a rather lavish lifestyle for your retirement years. That's okay, as long as you understand that you need to save today to make such a retirement life possible.

How Much Will You Need to Save?

Now you are ready to calculate just how much you'll need to save for retirement. We have supplied the number charts you need to convert current dollars into future dollars. Use current dollars and refer to the appropriate factor chart, as specified. You'll find the factor charts on the pages following.

1 _____ Total annual retirement income needed. This is the expense number you calculated in the preceding exercise. Or you can take your current pre-tax total annual income and multiply it by 0.8 to get this number.

SUBTRACT

2 _____ Annual Social Security retirement benefits

SUBTRACT

3 _____ Estimated income from pension plan (This does not include IRAs, 401(k)s, or profit-sharing plans.)

4 _____ Retirement income needed in current dollars

MULTIPLY LINE 4 BY FACTOR "A"

5 _____ Retirement income needed, adjusted for inflation

MULTIPLY LINE 5 BY FACTOR "B"

6 _____ Savings needed to fund income for retirement period

MULTIPLY LINE 3 BY FACTOR "A"

7 _____ Additional savings needed to maintain the purchasing power of your pension, not taking inflation into consideration

MULTIPLY LINE 7 BY FACTOR "C"

8 _____ Savings needed to maintain purchasing power of your pension, taking inflation into consideration

ADD LINE 6 PLUS LINE 8

9 _____ Total savings needed at beginning of retirement

#10 _____ Assets available to fund your retirement (This includes the *current* value of your IRAs, profit-sharing plans, 401(k)s and other personal investments.)

MULTIPLY LINE 10 BY FACTOR "D"

11 _____ Value of line 10 assets at retirement

LINE 9 MINUS LINE 11

#12 _____ Additional savings required at retirement

Is line #12 a negative number? If it is, you have already saved enough for your retirement. Keep your retirement funds invested and free from taxes and enjoy, enjoy, enjoy your other income.

Welcome to reality for those who got a positive number—and for 99.9 percent of the population, it will be a positive number. This means you need to start saving more for your retirement.

How much more will you need to save each year? Multiply Line 12 by Factor E to get the answer.

Getting There

Way short of the money to fund your retirement? Don't despair if you need to save $5,000 a year but you are now socking away only $2,500. Save the $2,500 you have available and consider making some adjustments. Take a hard look at what you are spending. If you cut $50 from your spending each week, you'll have $2,600 more at the end of the year to fund your retirement plan.

Earmark Salary Raises for Retirement

Whatever extra you can save now can translate into much bigger amounts—once you invest the money—when it comes time to retire because those investments compound. Moreover, your income between now and when you retire may rise significantly.

Make sure you plow a larger percentage of those heftier payroll checks into a retirement savings plan. Let's say you now are saving 10 percent of your income for retirement. When you get a 15 percent salary increase, start saving 12 percent rather than just 10 percent for retirement. You will be surprised at how quickly your money grows.

Factor A

This factor adjusts for inflation, which is assumed to be at 4 percent. While inflation may rise or fall from year to year, the 4 percent factor is used by most financial planners because it comes closest to the long-term level.

Years to Retirement	Factor A
1	1.04
2	1.08
3	1.12
4	1.17
5	1.22
6	1.27
7	1.32
8	1.37
9	1.42
10	1.48
11	1.54
12	1.60
13	1.67
14	1.73
15	1.80
16	1.87
17	1.95
18	2.03
19	2.11
20	2.19
21	2.28
22	2.37
23	2.46
24	2.56
25	2.67
26	2.77
27	2.88
28	3.00
29	3.12

30	3.24
31	3.37
32	3.51
33	3.65
34	3.79
35	3.95
36	4.10
37	4.27
38	4.44
39	4.62
40	4.80

Factor B

Use this factor to calculate the savings you will need at retirement. The longer you think you will be retired, the more money you will need. Delay your retirement and you'll need less.

You also need to determine the rate of return you think you will earn. If you go with low-risk investments, you'll get a lower rate of return. Aggressive growth funds are designed to give you the highest rate of return over the long term. Income and income-and-growth funds are in the middle. Inflation is assumed to be 4 percent.

	Rates of Return			
Retirement Period	6%	8%	10%	12%
20 years	16.79	14.31	12.36	10.82
25 years	20.08	16.49	13.82	11.81
30 years	23.07	18.30	14.93	12.48
35 years	25.79	19.79	15.76	12.95
40 years	28.26	21.03	16.39	13.28

Factor C

This is the factor to calculate the capital you'll need to maintain the spending power of your pension, if you have one. Inflation is assumed to be 4 percent.

Retirement Period	Rates of Return			
	6%	8%	10%	12%
20 years	4.63	3.70	3.00	2.45
25 years	6.53	4.96	3.84	3.02
30 years	8.48	6.14	4.56	3.46
35 years	10.42	7.21	5.15	3.80
40 years	12.31	8.15	5.63	4.04

Factor D

This gives you the growth factor of your savings to retirement. Notice the huge pay-off you get when you take more risk and get a higher rate of return. Saving for 21 years at 12 percent gets you more than saving for 40 years at 6 percent. Take the risk and you put yourself in a position to get the reward.

Years to Retirement	Growth Factors			
	6%	8%	10%	12%
1	1.06	1.08	1.10	1.12
2	1.12	1.17	1.21	1.25
3	1.19	1.26	1.33	1.40
4	1.26	1.36	1.46	1.57
5	1.34	1.47	1.61	1.76
6	1.42	1.49	1.77	1.97
7	1.50	1.71	1.95	2.21
8	1.59	1.85	2.14	2.48
9	1.69	2.00	2.36	2.77
10	1.79	2.16	2.59	3.11
11	1.90	2.33	2.85	3.48
12	2.01	2.52	3.14	3.90
13	2.13	2.72	3.45	4.36
14	2.26	2.94	3.80	4.89
15	2.40	3.17	4.18	5.47

16	2.54	3.43	4.59	6.13
17	2.69	3.70	5.05	6.87
18	2.85	4.00	5.56	7.69
19	3.03	4.32	6.12	8.61
20	3.21	4.66	6.73	9.65
21	3.40	5.03	7.40	10.80
22	3.60	5.44	8.14	12.10
23	3.82	5.87	8.95	13.55
24	4.05	6.34	9.85	15.18
25	4.29	6.85	10.83	17.00
26	4.55	7.40	11.92	19.04
27	4.82	8.00	13.11	21.32
28	5.11	8.63	14.42	23.88
29	5.42	9.32	15.86	26.75
30	5.74	10.06	17.45	29.96
31	6.09	10.87	19.19	33.56
32	6.45	11.74	21.11	37.58
33	6.84	12.68	23.22	42.09
34	7.25	13.69	25.55	47.14
35	7.69	14.79	28.10	52.80
36	8.15	15.97	30.91	59.14
37	8.64	17.25	34.00	66.23
38	9.15	18.63	37.40	74.18
39	9.70	20.12	41.14	83.08
40	10.29	21.72	45.26	93.05

Factor E

This factor is used to compute how much more you need to save if you delay your retirement savings program. Start early and save a little now, so you won't have to save a huge chunk of your income as you get closer to retirement.

	Savings Factor			
Years to Retirement	6%	8%	10%	12%
1	1.000	1.000	1.000	1.000
2	0.485	0.481	0.476	0.472
3	0.314	0.308	0.302	0.296

4	0.229	0.222	0.215	0.209
5	0.177	0.170	0.164	0.157
6	0.143	0.136	0.130	0.123
7	0.119	0.112	0.105	0.099
8	0.101	0.094	0.087	0.081
9	0.087	0.080	0.074	0.068
10	0.076	0.069	0.063	0.057
11	0.067	0.060	0.054	0.048
12	0.059	0.053	0.047	0.041
13	0.053	0.047	0.041	0.036
14	0.048	0.041	0.036	0.031
15	0.042	0.037	0.031	0.027
16	0.039	0.033	0.028	0.023
17	0.035	0.030	0.025	0.020
18	0.032	0.027	0.022	0.018
19	0.030	0.024	0.020	0.016
20	0.027	0.022	0.017	0.014
21	0.025	0.020	0.016	0.012
22	0.023	0.018	0.014	0.011
23	0.021	0.016	0.013	0.010
24	0.020	0.015	0.011	0.008
25	0.018	0.014	0.010	0.007
26	0.017	0.013	0.009	0.007
27	0.016	0.011	0.008	0.006
29	0.014	0.010	0.007	0.005
30	0.013	0.009	0.006	0.004
31	0.012	0.008	0.005	0.004
32	0.011	0.007	0.005	0.003
33	0.010	0.007	0.004	0.003
34	0.010	0.006	0.004	0.003
35	0.009	0.006	0.004	0.002
36	0.008	0.005	0.003	0.002
37	0.008	0.005	0.003	0.002
38	0.007	0.005	0.003	0.002
39	0.007	0.004	0.002	0.001
40	0.006	0.004	0.002	0.001

Your Spending and Savings Plan

If putting yourself on a budget seems akin to locking yourself into a prison cell, try this mental trick: Put yourself on a spending plan so you can save more. Just plug in the numbers for how you currently are spending—and hopefully saving—your money.

If you don't know the exact amount you are spending, just estimate. You can fine-tune the numbers as you become more comfortable with your spending and savings plan.

Take a look at how you are spending your money now. Can you find some ways to save? Plug those numbers into the column marked "Goal." You may be surprised at how easy it is to save more when you get a fix on what you are spending now.

INCOME	Current	Goal
Take-home salary after taxes and deductions	_____	_____
Take-home salary after taxes and deductions (second job or second income if you are married)	_____	_____
Other income: (from rental property, trust income, alimony, child support)	_____	_____
Tax refunds	_____	_____
Trusts	_____	_____
Interest & dividends	_____	_____
EXPENSES	**Current**	**Goal**
Savings (Pay yourself first!)	_____	_____
Emergency fund	_____	_____
Retirement accounts (IRAs, 401(k)s, Keoghs, etc.)	_____	_____
Investments	_____	_____

College education (You may be
able to use a part of your
401(k) plan for this)   _____   _____

Housing: _____   _____

    Mortgage/rent   _____   _____

    Electricity   _____   _____

    Gas/oil   _____   _____

    Water   _____   _____

    Maintenance & repairs   _____   _____

    Property taxes   _____   _____

    Homeowner's insurance   _____   _____

    Health insurance   _____   _____

Transportation   _____   _____

    Car payments   _____   _____

    Car insurance   _____   _____

Loans   _____   _____

    Bank loans   _____   _____

    Personal loans   _____   _____

    Education loans/expenses   _____   _____

    Home equity loans   _____   _____

Telephone (basic local and
long-distance service)   _____   _____

Groceries   _____   _____

    Food   _____   _____

    Household   _____   _____

Cleaning items   _____   _____

Personal care   _____   _____

Toiletries   _____   _____

Haircuts, facials   _____   _____

Clothing   _____   _____

    Adults   _____   _____

    Children   _____   _____

    Laundry & dry cleaning   _____   _____

Medical   _____   _____

Dental   _____   _____

Credit card accounts   _____   _____

    Auto   _____   _____

    Department store   _____   _____

    General   _____   _____

Transportation   _____   _____

    Gasoline   _____   _____

    Commuting costs   _____   _____

    Car maintenance (tune-up, new tires)   _____   _____

    Parking/public transportation   _____   _____

Licenses   _____   _____

Communications   _____   _____

    Telephone (special features)   _____   _____

    Cellular phone   _____   _____

    Pager   _____   _____

    Internet provider   _____   _____

Children   _____   _____

    Child care   _____   _____

School supplies/field trips _____   _____

Toys _____   _____

Clubs/lessons _____   _____

Pets _____   _____

Food _____   _____

Veterinarian _____   _____

Major Appliance Purchases _____   _____

Maintenance _____   _____

Furniture Purchases _____   _____

Maintenance _____   _____

Entertainment _____   _____

Eating out _____   _____

Meals _____   _____

Miscellaneous _____   _____

Concerts/theater tickets _____   _____

Movies _____   _____

Videocassette rentals _____   _____

Subscriptions _____   _____

Books, magazines, newspapers _____   _____

Hobbies _____   _____

Vacations _____   _____

Special holidays _____   _____

Easter/Passover _____   _____

Mother's Day _____   _____

Father's Day _____   _____

Fourth of July _____   _____

Halloween	_____	_____
Thanksgiving	_____	_____
Christmas/Hanukkah	_____	_____
New Year's Eve	_____	_____
Gifts	_____	_____
Friends & Family	_____	_____
Holidays	_____	_____
Birthday celebrations	_____	_____
Visits to out-of town family	_____	_____
Charitable/religious/political contributions	_____	_____
TOTAL	_____	_____

What Are Your Net Assets?

Your net worth is far, far greater than your net assets. Your worth is the sum of all your talents, your ambitions, the emotional gifts you bestow upon your friends and family, and the time you give to others. These are precious and will multiply as you grow older. Know them, but don't try to calculate them.

Your financial net assets, though, can be computed. Add up your financial assets, subtract your liabilities and you have a number that represents your net assets. Here is a worksheet to help you get started.

NET ASSET STATEMENT

Assets		Liabilities	
Checking account	$ _____	Mortgage	$ _____
Savings account	$ _____	Credit card balances	$ _____
Money market funds	$ _____	Car loans	$ _____
Life insurance cash values	$ _____	Bank loans	$ _____
Stocks/bonds	$ _____	School loans	$ _____
Mutual funds	$ _____	Alimony	$ _____
Certificates of deposit	$ _____	Other debt	$ _____
IRAs, Keoghs, 401(k)s	$ _____	Income tax	$ _____
Pension	$ _____	Real estate tax	$ _____
Real estate (home)	$ _____	TOTAL LIABILITIES	$ _____
Real estate (rental, vacation)	$ _____	TOTAL NET WORTH	$ _____
Cars	$ _____		
Jewelry, art, other valuables	$ _____		
TOTAL ASSETS	$ _____		

Calculator Off, Computer On

It's time now to turn off your calculator and turn on your computer to discover all the information you can get from cruising the Internet. The next chapter will tell you how you can access other people's information to help you fashion your retirement plan and keep it on track.

YOU CAN *leverage* your way *through* CYBERSPACE

CHAPTER TWELVE
This book helps you fashion your retirement plan. Use the **Internet** *to help you fill in some blanks. Learn where to go to get information about such things as mutual funds, which insurance companies get the highest ratings, and how to report shady* **deals.**

More is not always better. Nowhere is that truer than in cyberspace, where millions of messages and bits of information reside. Use any search engine to access the general topic of "retirement planning" and you'll get thousands of references. Spending too much time with all this information is only likely to confuse you.

Through the Internet you can access useful information about retirement planning, such as investing tips, how specific investments have fared, which insurance companies get the highest ratings, and how to report shady investment schemes.

Fraudbusters—Press Delete on Cyberscams

The Internet, with its online investment bulletin boards, has opened a rich vein of opportunity for an age-old problem: financial scams. Here are a few recent cases:

• A Michigan man on Prodigy's investment bulletin board, Money Talk, touted a mutual fund he said he managed. Two investors sent him a total of $101,000, only to learn that no such fund existed and the man was not a licensed broker.

• A message on an Internet bulletin board promised people an easy $50,000 in 60 days. It turned out to be a cyberspace chain letter.

• Over 20,000 investors coughed up nearly $200 each to get in on the ground floor of a worldwide telephone lottery pitched on America Online's Investor Network. Investors supposedly could make even more money by signing on other investors. The U.S. government—specifically the Securities and Exchange Commission—stopped the scam, a classic—and totally illegal—pyramid scheme.

• Messages on Prodigy's Money Talk urged subscribers to buy into a nutrition company with a hot new bodybuilding product. Turned out the messages were being orchestrated by a convicted swindler who owned stock in a company with ties to the nutrition firm. Over a five-month period, the price of the stock shot up from 38 cents to $7.50, thanks to all those people buying shares. The swindler was eventually caught and convicted. The value of the shares plummeted.

Ponzi schemes, penny-stock frauds, and other dubious financial schemes have invaded the Internet. Swindlers, con artists, and rapscallions can contact more people more quickly and less expensively than they can by the traditional telephone calling method.

Screening every message on these investment bulletin boards is an impossible task, and the online services do not guarantee the quality of the investments being touted on their bulletin boards. So the onus falls on you, the cyberspace traveler, to steer clear of these tricksters. If you like to browse these services on the Internet looking for investment opportunities, follow the same advice you would for any other investment opportunity offered by telephone, by mail, or in person.

• Be leery of extravagant claims. If it is too good to be true, it probably is.

• Don't get taken in by catchy headlines: "You Can't Lose" (of course you can and probably will); "Easy Cash" (for the con artists taking your money); "Big Bucks" (for the scammer, but less bucks for you); "Make Money Fast" (not for you, for the other guy).

• Don't be pressured into buying.

• Never buy something based solely on the information you pull off the bulletin board. Request printed information. Check out the offering with your state securities agency. The investment must be registered in the state where you live to be legally sold to you.

• Remember, just as with someone on the telephone, the person on the bulletin board may not be who he or she claims to be or to represent.

• Never give out your address, telephone number, credit card, or Social Security number.

So strap on your fraud-detectors before you travel the Internet. That way you will avoid having a cyberscam accident.

Use this book to help you fashion your overall retirement plan and the Internet to help you fill in some blanks.

Consider the Source

The most reliable and unbiased sites are generated by educational institutions and government agencies. All the other sites are generated by:

- People who want to sell you something. Insurance, brokerage, and mutual fund companies—no matter how aboveboard and solid they may be—want to sell you investments. Associations want you to join. Publications want you to subscribe. That is their business. Your business is keeping as much of your own money as possible so you'll have the dollars to make investments for your retirement plan.

- People who want to impress you with how clever or smart they are. Chat rooms are notorious for this. Do remember that your retirement plan is about your goals, not someone else's. The plan you put into place should fit your needs and aspirations. Don't let chat groups deter you from the steady and consistent investing plan you have created.

- People who want to scam, swindle, and bamboozle you.

With that warning firmly established, the Internet can act as your amigo number three—good old leverage. In this case, rather than using other people's money, you will be using other people's information to serve your purposes, not theirs.

The trick in using the Internet is to get information that's both free and reliable. Remember that unreliable information is worse than no information at all because it gives you the illusion that you are informed.

Resource Sites Galore

There are thousands of Internet sites with information related to retirement planning. Here are just a few of the sites you may find interesting in helping you keep your retirement plan on track.

Financenter on the Web

A visit to this instructive and fun site (http://www.financenter.com) will let you scope into a number of different sections that provide solid information and exercises on the subject of personal finance and retirement planning. You can plug in numbers about your specific situation—age, income, marital status, and the like—and discover how much you need to save to become a millionaire or how much you need to pay per month to bring your credit card balance down to zero.

Here's a rundown of the Financenter sections and what you'll find in each.

- *Homes:* How much can you borrow on your income? How much will your monthly payments be for a specific mortgage at a specific rate? Submit an application to get preapproved for a mortgage level.

- *Autos:* Should you lease or buy? How much will your monthly payments be to purchase a car? Calculate whether it's smarter to take the rebate money or to go for a low-rate loan.

- *Credit cards:* How long will it take to pay off your balance? Should you consolidate your debts?

- *Budget:* How much should you set aside for an emergency fund? What's it worth to reduce your spending? Is it smarter for you to pay off your debt or to invest?

- *Savings:* How much will your current savings be worth in future years? How much do you need to invest now to become a millionaire at a specific age?

- *Stocks:* Calculate the yield on your stock investments. Which is a better investment for you—growth stocks or income stocks?

- *Bonds:* How will rate changes affect the value of your bond investments? Calculate the yield to maturity on your bonds.

Annual Reports for Free on the Web

Want to get an annual report of a company in which you are considering investing? The Public Register's Annual Report Service site (http://www.prars.com) allows you to order annual reports from some 3,200 companies for free. Fill in the information for free and within 24 hours the report you want will be shipped to you through the mail.

EDGAR

EDGAR stands for Electronic Data Gathering, Analysis, and Retrieval system. This site lets you see the documents that companies must file with the Securities and Exchange Commission (SEC). While companies are not required to file their annual reports with the SEC, they must file a 10-K form which contains most of the information in an annual report.

Allow some time to access this page. It's popular, so you might have to wait a while before the information pops onto your screen.

You can access EDGAR through a number of different addresses. Here are a few:

http://edgar.whowhere.com/

http://edgar.stern.nyu.edu/mutual.html

http://edgar.stern.nyu.edu/edgar.html

Securities and Exchange Commission Online

You pay your taxes, so you might as well get as much from the government as you can when it comes to information about planning for retirement. The SEC site (http://www.sec.gov) will also get you to EDGAR.

The site is also filled with general investing information about risk, mutual funds, and questions to ask someone who may be trying to sell you a mutual fund.

The SEC site gives you information about lodging complaints about your investments if you suspect fraud or shady practices.

Every state has a state securities regulatory office which handles such complaints, as well. You can access a list of all 50 state regulators through http://.sec.gov/consumer/state.htm.

National Fraud Information Center Online

This site (http://www.nfic.inter.net) provides information on over 800 different types of scams. You can report suspected fraud or scams directly through e-mail found at http://www.nfic.inter.net/nficmail.htm.

Federal Trade Commission Online

This is an alternative site (http://www.ftc.gov/bcp/conline/conline/htm) covering fraud for investment and noninvestment problems in such areas as life insurance, home improvement scams, and door-to-door sales.

The FTC site also features a section on "66 Ways to Save Money" and consumer tips on dozens of subjects such as life insurance, credit cards, and automobiles. You can also cyberspace through the steps you need to take for "How to Write a Wrong."

Insurance Sites

There are a slew of sites that provide information about insurance. To get insurance quotes, check out the site at http://iquote.com.

General information about insurance and insurance firms can be found at http://www.insure.com/.

Here you can review the different types of life insurance, a glossary of terms, and a list of questions to ask someone trying to sell you a policy. You also can access how individual insurance companies are rated by two independent ratings firms—Standard & Poor's and Duff & Phelps.

Make sure you have the full name of the insurance company you are investigating. A major insurance firm may have separate companies in each of the 50 states. Each of these state firms may have its own insurance rating.

Mutual Fund Sites

It's hard to find a mutual fund company that does not have a home page. Mutual fund company home pages usually provide a rundown of investment offerings, let you get stock market quotes, and supply information on interest rates.

NETworth

You can get a good list of mutual funds at this site (http://networth.galt.com) organized by the Quicken Financial Network, plus a wealth of information on over 5,000 of them. Try searching for mutual funds according to performance, objectives, and cost.

Some of this site's best features include the Mutual Fund Market Manager, a Fund Search function, and a Meet the Experts page. You can also keep up-to-date with the mutual fund market in the Market Outlook area where you can find timely articles on relevant market topics.

Fidelity Online

This site (http://www.fid/inv.com/personal investing/) gives you a lot of different and interesting options.

Try the Investor Toolbox, where you can enter information about your specific situation to discover how much you need to save to reach your retirement goal.

The Asset Allocation category on Fidelity's Web site provides sample asset allocation portfolios and helps you devise an asset allocation that works for you. It also suggests specific bond and stock mutual funds that would be appropriate investments for special asset allocations.

The 401(k) section is useful in providing general information related to these retirement investment plans. Also check out Fidelity's *Stages* magazine on this Web site.

Remember, of course, that Fidelity is interested in getting you to invest with the company. Fidelity's specific suggestions, though, may serve as an illustration of the types of investments you should be examining for the asset allocation that fits your goals.

Brokerage Firm Sites

Like mutual fund companies, brokerage firms, too, have discovered the value of promoting their products and services via the Internet. Of course, some home pages are more helpful than others.

Merrill Lynch Online

This site (http://www.ml.com) will keep you occupied for an entire rainy weekend. Here you will find retirement planning terms and concepts, a section on savings, and an Investors Learning Center. The Web site also provides forms you can use to help you get organized when it comes to spending money, calculating your net assets, and constructing a household budget.

Scan the information on seminars sponsored by Merrill Lynch. Attend one in your area and you may get a free meal with the investment information you receive at the seminar.

Ceres Securities Online

If you are only interested in getting to the nitty-gritty of actually investing online, this might be a good place for you. Ceres (http://www.ceres.com) offers inexpensive transaction fees but not a lot of information. Use them only if you feel you are ready to take the plunge without a lot of outside direction. You won't find much help from the folks at Ceres, but you will be able to track your portfolio, place orders, and get quick stock quotes.

E*TRADE Online

This is another online broker, offering the bare minimum of investment services. E*Trade (http://www.etrade.com) features a Stock Market Game that allows new investors to practice investing without actually putting any of their own money on the line. It's a neat way to get comfortable with the market before taking the plunge.

Charles Schwab

Charles Schwab, one of the most well-known of the discount brokerage houses, can also be found on the Web (http://www.schwab.com). You can obtain Schwab's proprietary investment software that will allow you to invest online and keep track of your portfolio.

Clueless about Retirement Gives the Plan

The basic and most important information for creating your retirement plan is contained in this book. Internet information merely provides details for monitoring your plan and checking out specific investments.

When it comes to chat rooms, keep in mind that these conversation sites most often focus on picking hot stocks. But retirement planning is not about picking the hot stocks; it's about a long-term program that is founded upon sensible asset allocation. That means getting the right mix of stocks and bonds into place and letting the investments work. It also means diversifing your money among different investments and saving steadily and consistently.

Do that, and you will most likely discover the chat rooms you visit are more entertaining than informative.

THAT'S a WRAP!

CHAPTER THIRTEEN

Get started on your retirement plan even if there are some decisions you have yet to make. The sooner you get the ball **rolling,** *the easier it will be for you to meet your goals. You can always revise your strategy as you* **go along.**

The overarching key to success for any project is to have a vision and goals which are uniquely yours. Maintain a vision of your retirement plan, and you will be able to keep your plan on track no matter what comes up.

A Quick Recap

Here's a recap of how to translate that vision into reality. You'll need:

• Savings. These are your main ingredients.

- A plan or plans where your savings can grow tax-deferred. These are your recipes.

- Different types of investments to put into those tax-deferred plans. This is the meat and potatoes of your retirement strategy.

Remember Your Three Amigos

Your three amigos—asset allocation, diversification, and leverage—will provide the framework for many of the decisions you will make over the years concerning the type of plans—401(k), IRAs, and Keoghs, for instance—you will be using and the type of investments you will be making.

A steady and consistent plan of savings and investing will get you to your goal. The sooner you start, the more money you'll have when you retire. Remember, early savings that are invested earn more over time than later savings. Moreover, the sooner you begin, the more time you will have to correct any mistakes you may make along the way.

Don't get discouraged if one of your investments turns out to be a bummer. Even Spielberg has had a box-office dog here and there.

The important thing is to maintain your savings plan. That means always pay yourself first. Then you just invest those savings regularly—when the markets go down and when they are rising.

Take Charge

As you fine-tune your plan, you will be seeking and getting advice and input from a host of different people and institutions such as bankers, insurance agents, securities brokers, financial planners, and the like. Keep in mind that these helpers can provide valuable information, but you are always the one in charge of your plan.

Don't be afraid to ask questions. No query you make is a dumb one. Just make sure you understand the answers you get.

Moreover, it's your responsibility to make sure that your plan is progressing according to your screenplay. If your helpers are rude or patronizing or just not there when you have a question, let them know that you are prepared to find someone else or some other institution to be a part of your retirement plan. These people work for you, so don't be afraid to tell them what you want and, if necessary, to fire them if they are not performing for you.

A Plan with Pleasures

Creating a retirement plan that works for you will give you a sense of security that can spill over to other parts of your life. Knowing that you are taking the steps to take care of yourself will make you feel more independent and effective when it comes to dealing with your boss and your clients.

It also serves as a powerful example to your children that being responsible for oneself creates a sense of well-being. Moreover, a sound retirement plan takes a burden off your kids because they will be assured that they do not need to worry about taking care of you in your retirement years.

Finally, fashioning your own retirement plan gives you the opportunity to live all the years of life with the resources you need to grow emotionally and spiritually. With money worries on the back burner, you can translate the knowledge and experiences of youth into the wisdom you will rely upon to truly relish every moment of your retirement.

YOUR ENDURING LEGACY

Fired up to start amassing a financial **fortune** for your retirement years and some big bucks to leave as a legacy to those you love? Remember that the greatest gift you can give to those you love is not your money but your time.

While a **gift** of $10,000 would be most welcomed by your children or grandchildren, the memories of the time you spend with them will be a far greater legacy. Think about it. What do you remember of your grandparents? The money they gave you? Of course, you do.

But when you are discouraged and feeling blue, what gives you the support to pick up the pieces and try again? The memory of the money you received—or the memory of the holiday dinner at your grandmother's house, the baseball outing with your grandfather, or the kind words and love you received from both? It's not the **money**, but the time you give to others that endures.

GLOSSARY

aggressive growth fund: A mutual fund that invests in companies that are newer and more on the cutting edge than growth companies. These are relatively high-risk funds with potential for tremendous price increases and high rates of failure.

aggressive growth stock: Stock in a company that is small, but rapidly expanding, giving the investor the opportunity to attain above-average returns.

annual report: A document presented to stockholders once a year that includes information about how the company is doing. It contains the balance sheet, income statement, and statement of cash flows as well as discussions about the business.

annuity: An investment that guarantees a fixed income for the remainder of a person's life. In return for the payment of a premium, you are guaranteed an annual income beginning at a designated age and continuing for the rest of your life.

appreciate: To increase in value.

asset: Something of value, i.e., cash, inventory, equipment, or real estate.

asset allocation: A strategy that divides investments among a variety of types of instruments and rates of return (and risk).

bankruptcy: The condition in which corporations or individuals legally declare that they cannot meet their financial obligations.

bear market: A prolonged period of falling stock prices. Opposite of a bull market.

beneficiary: The person named to receive money or property after the death of the original owner.

blue-chip stock: The stock of a large, relatively stable, well-established company, named after the blue chips in a poker game, the chips with the highest value.

bond: An interest-bearing debt.

bond fund: A mutual fund that invests in bonds.

Bridal Registry Account: A Federal Housing Administration program that enables gift-givers to deposit money into an account to be used for a home.

broker: A company that, or an individual who, facilitates a stock transaction but does not own the stock at the end of the sale.

budget: A systematic plan for spending and saving money over a definite period of time, based on income and expenses.

bull market: A prolonged period of rising stock prices. Opposite of a bear market.

capital gain: Money earned by selling an asset for a profit.

cash equivalents: Short-term, highly liquid securities which can be turned into cash quickly, such as short-term certificates of deposit, money market funds, and Treasury bills.

certificate of deposit (CD): An arrangement whereby a depositor receives a fixed rate of return on a principal that has been deposited for a specific time period. Because there is a penalty for early withdrawal of the principal, the interest rate is usually more than a savings account. CDs are issued by banks, credit unions, and savings and loan associations, and are generally insured up to $100,000 by the FDIC (Federal Deposit Insurance Corporation) or the Federal Savings & Loan Insurance Corporation.

Certified Financial Planner (CFP): A financial adviser who has taken courses, passed exams, and been certified by the Institute of Certified Financial Planners.

Certified Public Accountant: (CPA): An accountant who has passed a series of exams and met state requirements.

collateral: The assets put up by a borrower as a pledge for a loan. The collateral can be taken by the lender if the loan is not repaid.

collectible: An asset of limited supply that is bought in the hopes that it will increase in value.

commission: The fee charged by a broker to negotiate the purchase or sale of a security.

common stock: A type of stock which entitles the owner to have voting rights in the corporation and a claim to what remains after all the creditors and preferred stock-holders have been paid, if the company goes out of business.

compound interest: Interest that is earned from both the principal and the interest accumulated on the principal.

consolidated loan: A loan made to replace two or more outstanding loans.

convertible bond: A debt instrument that can be converted into a stock.

corporate bond: A debt instrument issued by a corporation as a means of raising money.

credit: The power to borrow money based on reputation for repayment, net income, and assets.

credit union: A nonprofit institution that provides banking services to its members who share a common bond.

custodian: An organization like a bank that maintains an account for someone.

deductible: 1) Describes an expense that can be used to reduce the amount of income tax liability. 2) The amount of money an insurance policyholder must pay before the insurance company provides benefits.

defined benefit plan: A pension plan in which the employer specifies the amount of payments to the employee at the time of retirement, rather than contributing regularly into the plan for the duration of the individual's employment.

defined contribution plan: A pension plan like a 401(k) in which an employer contributes specified scheduled payments into the plan.

deflation: The rate at which the real cost of goods and services declines in the economy.

devaluation: A reduction in the value of one currency compared with other currencies.

disability insurance: Insurance that pays the policyholder if he/she becomes unable to work due to an illness or injury.

diversification: An investment strategy that relies on distributing investments among a variety of securities to minimize risk.

dividend: A payment issued by a company that distributes part of its profits and earnings to shareholders.

dollar cost averaging: An investment strategy whereby an investor contributes equal amounts of money to an investment at regular intervals.

Federal Deposit Insurance Corporation (FDIC): A federal agency that insures deposits up to $100,000 at commercial banks.

Federal Housing Administration: A U.S. government-sponsored agency that insures mortgages.

Federal Insurance Contributions Act (FICA): U.S. government legislation that mandates employees contributions to the Social Security plan.

Federal Savings and Loan Insurance Corporation (FSLIC): A federal agency that insures deposits in savings and loans up to $100,000.

Federal Trade Commission (FTC): A U.S. government agency that regulates competitive markets with regard to discouraging monopolies and encouraging free trade.

financial planner: A person who provides advice about identifying financial goals and strategies for meeting them.

fixed-income investment: An investment that pays a steady income, like bonds or preferred stock.

fixed interest rate: An interest rate that remains constant for the length of the debt.

floating interest rate: An interest rate that changes at set intervals during the length of the debt.

401(k): A company-sponsored retirement plan.

fraud: Deception for personal gain by the means of false statements or actions.

futures contract: An agreement to take delivery or deliver a specific commodity (grains, metals, foreign currencies) on a particular date.

gross annual income: The total yearly receipts from an individual's work, business, and property before any deductions have been made for taxes or expenses.

growth and income fund: A mutual fund that invests in both growth and income companies.

growth and income stock: Equity in a company that has the potential for capital appreciation and pays dividends.

growth fund: A mutual fund that invests in young companies that have the potential to grow very quickly. They usually pay low or no dividends, and the value of the stock has the potential to rise or fall quickly.

growth stock: A stock that has the potential of increasing its price as the company expands and prospers.

home equity loan: A loan that allows homeowners to borrow 70 to 80 percent of the appraised value of their house, minus what is owed on it.

illiquid: Describes an investment that is difficult to convert to cash.

income fund: A mutual fund that invests in older, well-established companies that grow slowly but steadily and pay relatively large dividends.

Individual Retirement Account (IRA): A tax-deferred account into which employed individuals can make annual contributions of up to $2,000 and withdrawals without penalty after the age of 59 1/2.

inflation: The rate at which the real cost of goods and services rises in the economy.

interest: Payment for money that is borrowed.

Internal Revenue Service (IRS): The U.S. federal agency that collects taxes and administers the tax laws.

investment: Money you put into some form of property or security for income or profit, such as a home or pension plan.

junk bond: A debt security graded less than BBB. Because it is rated so low by the bond rating companies, it produces a higher yield, but it is also a high-risk investment.

Keogh plan: A retirement plan for self-employed individuals.

leverage: An investment technique whereby one uses other people's money or resources.

liquidate: To convert assets into cash.

liquidity: A term that describes how quickly and easily an investment can be converted to cash.

market risk: The danger that the stock market as a whole will decline.

market timing: The ability to predict when stock prices are going to start to rise or decline.

maturity: The time period of a loan.

money market account: Offered by banks, savings and loan institutions, and credit unions, these accounts are like checking accounts that pay interest. They are insured by the FDIC.

money market fund: A mutual fund that invests in short-term, low-risk nonequity securities such as commercial paper, Treasury bills, and certificates of deposit.

mortgage: A loan that is backed by property as security.

mortgage-backed security: A government bond that carries a higher risk and usually a higher rate of return than a U.S. Treasury bond. The investment is backed by mortgages that the government has insured.

mutual fund: An investment company that pools the resources of hundreds or thousands of individuals to enable them to diversify in a variety of investments, including stocks, bonds, and money markets.

net assets: The total assets minus the total liabilities of an individual or company.

net income: The money available after all taxes and expenses have been subtracted from gross income.

New York Stock Exchange (NYSE): The largest and most active stock market in the world.

option: A contract to buy or sell an asset (like shares of a stock) at a set price until a specific date.

penny stock: An inexpensive stock usually issued for new business ventures. Because the underlying companies are unknown and possibly unstable, the potential for fraud is high.

pension plan: An arrangement that allows an employer to pay retirement benefits to employees.

Ponzi scheme: An investment fraud named after Charles A. Ponzi who ran a large scam of this type in the 1920s. It works on a pyramid principle whereby early investors are paid off with money coming from succeeding waves of investors, who in turn lure more investors, the last of whom lose the most.

portfolio: A group of investments.

preferred stock: A type of stock that gives the stockholder first dibs over common stockholders to the dividends and assets of the company if the company goes out of business. Preferred stockholders are guaranteed fixed dividends but have no voting rights.

premium: A payment for an insurance policy.

profit-sharing plan: A plan offered by employers that allows employees to deposit a portion of the company's profits into a tax-deferred retirement account.

pyramid scheme: [See: Ponzi scheme.]

rate of return: A measure of the income that an investment will yield.

raw land: Land that is undeveloped.

real estate: Land and buildings.

Real Estate Investment Trust (REIT): A company that buys real estate or mortgages.

rider: An addition or option to a contract or insurance policy.

risk: The uncertainty of investment returns.

roll over: To reinvest funds from one account to another.

savings and loan: An institution that takes deposits and makes primarily real estate loans.

search engine: An Internet feature that enables the user to look for information.

Securities and Exchange Commission (SEC): The federal regulatory agency that oversees the securities markets and administers the securities laws.

share: A single unit of ownership in a corporation or mutual fund.

Social Security: The U.S. government-sponsored retirement plan.

speculation: The practice of purchasing stock based on its potential selling price instead of its actual value.

Standard & Poor's: A company that provides financial information including a stock index (S & P 500) and insurance ratings.

stock: A share of ownership in a corporation.

stock fund: A mutual fund that invests exclusively in equities.

stock market crash: An unusually large drop in the overall value of stock prices on a particular day.

tax bracket: A designation that determines what percentage of income must be paid in taxes. Theoretically, the more income an individual receives, the higher the tax bracket, and the larger the percentage of taxes due.

tax deduction: An expense, that when declared to the IRS, can be used to reduce the amount of taxes to be paid.

tax-deferred account: An account that contains funds that are not taxed until a later date.

tax shelter: An investment used for deferring, eliminating, or reducing income taxes.

10-K statement: A detailed analysis of a company's financial condition filed annually with the Securities and Exchange Commission.

10-Q statement: A company's financial report, less detailed than the 10-K, filed quarterly with the Securities and Exchange Commission.

term life insurance: A type of life insurance that covers a period of time.

trust: A legal arrangement that provides for an individual or an organization to manage money for someone else.

trustee-to-trustee transfer: A transaction in which an individual instructs an institution holding a retirement account to switch it to another institution. Because the individual does not take possession of the funds, the IRS imposes no penalty for the move and the money remains tax-deferred.

U.S. savings bond: A security issued by the U.S. Treasury, the interest of which is exempt from state and local taxes.

U.S. Treasury bill: A short-term debt security of the U.S. Treasury.

U.S. Treasury bond: A longer-term debt security of the U.S. Treasury.

U.S. Treasury note: An intermediate-term debt security of the U.S. Treasury.

universal life insurance: A type of insurance that enables the policyholder to purchase term insurance at a higher price and invest the difference in a tax-free account.

utility stock: Equity in gas, oil, electric, or other energy company.

vested right: An individual's claim to a share of some future benefit, such as a pension, toward which the individual has paid or earned credits.

volatility: An investment's price swings.

W-2 form: A statement from an individual's employer that details how much the individual earned in a given year, the amount of taxes that were withheld, and whether or not the individual is covered by a pension plan.

whole life insurance: A type of insurance that spans the policyholder's life.

yield: The amount of money you can expect to make from an investment.

zero coupon bond: A bond issued at a discount that increases in value as it approaches maturity, but provides no periodic interest payment.

RESOURCES

Books

The Adventure of Retirement: It's about More Than Just Money. Guild A. Fetridge (Prometheus Books, 1994).

The Beardstown Ladies' Common-Sense Investment Guide. The Beardstown Ladies' Investment Club with Leslie Whitaker (Hyperion, 1994).

The Beardstown Ladies' Stitch-in-Time Guide to Growing Your Nest Egg. The Beardstown Ladies' Investment Club with Robin Dellabough (Hyperion, 1996).

The Budget Kit, Second Edition. Judy Lawrence (Dearborn Financial Publishing, 1997).

Building Your Nest Egg with Your 401(k): A Guide to Help You Achieve Retirement Security. Lynn Brenner (Nolo Press, 1996).

Finding Your Financial Freedom: Every Woman's Guide to Success. Joyce Ward (Dearborn Financial Publishing, 1997).

50 Great Investments for the 21st Century. Diego Veitia (Dearborn Financial Publishing, 1997).

Kiplinger's 12 Steps to a Worry-Free Retirement. Daniel Kehrer (Times Books, 1995).

Money Lessons for a Lifetime: Stories, Observations and Tips on Living a Prosperous Life. James Jorgensen (Dearborn Financial Publishing, 1997).

The Motley Fool Investment Guide. David and Tom Gardner (Simon & Schuster, 1996).

Mutual Fund Investing on the Internet. Peter Crane (Ap Professional, 1997).

The 100 Best Mutual Funds to Own in America, Second Edition. Gene Walden (Dearborn Financial Publishing, 1997).

The Vanguard Retirement Investing Guide: Charting Your Course to a Secure Retirement. The Vanguard Group of Investment Companies (Irwin Professional Publishing, 1995).

Magazines and Newspapers

Barron's. 200 Liberty Street, New York, NY 10281, (800) 568-7625, $145/yr., weekly.

BusinessWeek. 1221 Avenue of the Americas, New York, NY 10020, (800) 635-1200, $49.95/yr., weekly (51 issues).

Financial World. 1328 Broadway, New York, NY 10001, (800) 829-5916, $27/yr. (18 issues).

Forbes. 60 Fifth Avenue, New York, NY 10011, (800) 888-9896, $57/yr., biweekly.

Fortune. P.O. Box 60001, Tampa, FL 33660, (800) 621-8000, $57/yr., biweekly.

Inc. P.O. Box 54129, Boulder, CO 80332, (800) 234-0999, $19/yr. (18 issues).

Individual Investor. P.O. Box 680, Mt. Morris, IL 61054, (800) 383-5901, $22.95/yr., monthly.

Investor's Business Daily. 12655 Beatrice Street, Los Angeles, CA 90066, (800) 831-2525, $189/yr, daily.

Kiplinger's Personal Finance. 3401 East-West Highway, Hyattsville, MD 20782, (800) 544-0155, $19.95/yr., monthly.

Money. P.O. Box 60001, Tampa, FL 33660, (800) 633-9970, $39.95/yr. (13 issues).

The New York Times. P.O. Box 2047, South Hackensack, NJ 07606, (800) 631-2500, $374.40/yr., daily.

Smart Money. P.O. Box 7538, Red Oak, IA 51591, (800) 444-4204, $24/yr., monthly.

The Wall Street Journal. 200 Liberty Street, New York, NY 10011, (800) 568-7625, $175/yr., five days per week delivery.

Worth. P.O. Box 55420, Boulder, CO 80322, (800) 777-1851, $18/yr. (ten issues).

Newsletters and Reports

Morningstar Mutual Funds. 225 West Wacker Drive, Chicago, IL 60606, (800) 735-0700, $425/yr., biweekly.

The Value Line Investment Survey. P.O. Box 3988, New York, NY 10008, (800) 833-0046, $570/yr., weekly.

Zacks Analyst Watch. Zacks Investment Research, 155 North Wacker Drive, Chicago, IL 60606, (800) 399-6659, $295/yr., bimonthly.

Online Resources

American Stock Exchange Web site, http://www.amex.com

Bloomberg Web site, http://www.bloomberg.com

BulletProof Investor's Web site, http://www.bulletproof.com

BusinessWeek Online Web site, http://www.mcgraw-hill.com/business-economics/bwol.htm

Ceres Securities Web site, http://www.ceres.com

Crain's Chicago Business Web site, http://www.bizpubs.org/chicago.htm

Doug Gerlach's Invest-O-Rama Web site, http://www.investorama.com

EDGAR Web site, http://edgar.whowhere.com/

E*TRADE Web site, http://www.etrade.com

Federal Trade Commission Web site, http: //www.ftc.gov

Fidelity Web site, http://www.fid- inv.com

Financenter Web site, http://www.financenter.com/

Hoover's Online Web site, http://www.hoovers.com

Internal Revenue Service Web site, http://www.irs.ustreas.gov

Investment Brokerages Guide Web site, http://www.cs.cmu.edu/~jdg/invest_^brokers/index.html

Motley Fool Web site, http://www.fool.com

Nasdaq Stock Market Web site, http://www.nasdaq.com

NETworth Web site, http://networth.galt.com

New York Stock Exchange Web site, http://www.nyse.com

New York Times Online Web site, http://www.nyt.com/

Quicken Financial Network Web site, http://www.qfn.com/index.html

Quote.com Web site, http://www.quote.com

Schwab Web site, http://www.schwab.com

Securities and Exchange Commission Web site, http://www.sec.gov

Silicon Investor Web site, http://www.techstocks.com

Stein Roe Web site, http://www.steinroe.com

Stock Smart Web site, http://www.stocksmart.com

Worth Web site, http://www.worth.com

Investment Clubs

National Association of Investors Corporation. 711 W. Thirteen-Mile Rd.,
Madison Heights, MI 48071, (810) 583-6242. For listings of local
investment clubs in your area.

Associations and Organizations

American Association of Individual Investors. 625 N. Michigan Ave., Suite
1900, Chicago, IL 60611, (312) 280-0170.
Web site: http://www.aaii.org/

American Stock Exchange. 86 Trinity Place, New York, NY 10006,
(212) 306-1000. Web site: http://www.amex.com

Dun & Bradstreet. 899 Eaton Ave., Bethlehem, PA 18025, (800) 234-
3867. Web site: http://www.dbisna.com/dbis/purchase/tpurchas.htm

Investment Company Institute. 1401 H Street N.W., Suite 1200,
Washington, DC 20005, (202) 326-5872.

Lipper Analytical Services. 74 Trinity Pl., New York, NY 10006,
(212) 393-1300. Web site: http://www.lipperweb.com

National Association of Investors Corp. P.O. 220, Royal Oak, MI 48068, (810) 583-6242.

National Association of Securities Dealers. 1818 N Streeet, N.W., Washington, DC 20036, (800) 289-9999. Web site: http://www.nasdr.com

National Center for Financial Education. P.O. Box 34070, San Diego, CA 92163, (619) 232-8811.

National Fraud Information Center. P.O. 65868, Washington, DC 20035, (800) 876-7060. Web site: http://www.fraud.org

New York Stock Exchange. 11 Wall Street, New York, NY 10005, (212) 656-3000. Web site: http://www.nyse.com

North American Securities Administrators Association. 1 Massachusetts Ave., N.W., Suite 310, Washington, DC 20001, (202) 737-0900.

Securities and Exchange Commission, Office of Investor Education & Assistance. 450 Fifth St., N.W. Washington, DC 20549, (202) 942-7040. Web site: http://www.sec.gov

INDEX

Access Research, 93
America Online, 156
Annual reports, 160
Annuities, 52, 111, 116
    fixed, 81, 111; payments, 112; switching, 112;
    tax advantages, 111; variable rate, 47, 111, 112
Antiques, 65
Art, 65
Asset
    allocation, 73–78, 84, 86, 102, 124, 126, 130,
    131, 162, 164, 166; calculating, 141, 152,
    153, 163
AT&T, 48

Baby boomers, 23, 24
Bánks, 92, 115
    Bridal Registry Accounts, 100; buying invest-
    ments from, 46, 123; checking accounts, 9, 52,
    75, 114, 153; direct deposits, 35; financial
    advisers, 114; insurance, 116, 118; IRAs, 64,
    65, 118, 129; loans, 114, 149; money market
    accounts, 52; mortgages, 99; mutual funds,
    117, 118; savings accounts, 52, 114, 153; U. S.
    savings bonds, 29; Wells Fargo, 47
Bear market, 56, 93
Better Business Bureau, 121
Blue-chip stocks, 51
Bonds, 4, 7, 27, 29, 46–48, 55, 81, 92, 114, 116,
153
    annuities, 112; asset allocation, 74–76, 164;
    AT&T, 48; buying from brokers, 117; corpo-
    rate, 51, 54, 55, 81; government, 25, 29, 52,

54, 55, 81; interest, 47, 49, 55, 56, 80, 131,
132; IRAs, 64, 65; junk, 51; maturity, 47, 55,
56, 159; mortgage-backed securities, 54; mutual funds, 47, 52, 54, 55, 64, 65, 75, 77, 81,
84; online sources, 159; prices, 56; reconfiguring your portfolio, 125–127; risk, 49, 131,
132; selling, 55, 129, 130; tax-free, 69; U.S.
savings, 25, 29; U.S. Treasury, 52; zero
coupon, 52
Bridal Registry Accounts, 100
Brokerage firms, 114, 115, 123, 166
    Charles Schwab, 164; choosing, 11, 14; fees,
    11, 14, 86–88, 128; insurance, 116; IRAs, 11,
    64, 65, 129; Merrill Lynch, 47, 60, 163; online
    sources, 163, 164; statements, 11
Budgets, 8, 9, 148, 159
    online sources, 163; single individuals, 133
Bull market, 56, 93
Cash management accounts, 115
Cash equivalents
    certificates of deposit, 48, 50, 53, 61, 65, 74,
    131, 153; money market funds, 48, 52, 61, 74,
    75, 131, 153
Capital gains, 98
Certificates of deposit, 48, 50, 74, 153
    401(k), 61; interest rates, 48, 131; early with-
    drawal penalties, 50; IRAs, 61, 65; liquidity,
    50; money market funds, 53
Certified Financial Planners, 72
Collectibles, 28, 51, 65
Company-sponsored retirement plans, 79
Compound interest, 33, 36, 38, 60, 82, 91

Commissions, 65
Consultants, 34
Convertible stocks and bonds, 47
Corporate downsizing, 10
Credit cards, 8, 40, 133, 150, 153, 161
  interest rate, 42, 43, 89; MasterCard, 43; minimum fee, 42; paying down balances, 35, 41, 43, 89, 159
Credit unions
  money market accounts, 52
Creditors, 9
Currency risk, 132
Custodian, 34, 128, 129

Debt, 23, 43, 82, 153
  asset allocation, 74, 75; bonds, 4, 7, 27, 29, 46–49, 51, 52, 54–56, 64, 65, 69, 75, 77, 80; consolidating loans, 39; convertible, 47; creditors, 9; diversification, 80; fixed rate, 42; floating rate, 42; investments, 4, 7, 27, 29, 46–49; 51, 52, 54, 55; market risk, 132; paying down, 7, 9, 35, 42, 43, 57, 138
Defined benefit plans, 69
  disadvantages of, 69, 70; Keoghs, 71, 72
Defined contribution plans, 19
  401(k) 2, 15, 34, 39, 59, 61, 67–72, 76, 78, 82, 83, 85, 86, 88, 89–96, 111, 141, 148, 153, 162, 166
Deflation, 80
Direct deposits, 32, 35
  bank, 35; 401(k), 34; IRA, 34
Diversification, 73, 79, 84, 129, 164
  comparing performance, 124; equities, 78, 81; 401(k), 166; fixed-income investments, 78, 81; insurance, 15; IRAs, 166; liquid versus illiquid investments, 78; Keoghs, 166; minimizing risk, 48, 124, 126, 127, 131, 132; real estate, 15, 102
Dividends, 47
  growth funds, 54; income funds, 54; reinvesting, 54
Dollar cost averaging, 82–85, 132
Duff & Phelps, 161

Earnings, 37
Employer contributions, 34, 61
  tax advantages, 61
Equity investments, 52, 56, 82, 92, 126, 129, 130
  asset allocation, 74–78; convertible, 47; deflation, 80; diversification, 78, 80, 81; dividends, 47; inflation, 56; interest rates, 56; IRAs, 65; market crash, 73; market fluctuations, 83; market timing, 76; Merrill Lynch, 47, 58; mutual funds, 47, 48, 51, 54, 65, 83; NYSE, 117; online sources, 159, 163, 164; real estate, 47; risk 79, 131, 132; shares, 55; shareholders, 47; stocks, 4, 7, 27, 29, 46, 48, 49, 52, 58, 84, 98, 112, 114, 116, 125, 130, 131, 153; transportation, 150; volatility of, 74, 76
E*TRADE, 164
Expenses
  calculating, 136, 139–152; children, 150; clothing, 150; collectibles, 28, 29; communications, 150; dental, 66, 150; emergency fund, 148; fixed, 8; groceries, 149; hobbies, 28; medical, 63, 66, 67, 150; retirement, 12, 24, 42, 136, 137–140; savings, 148; transportation, 150; utilities, 149

Federal Housing Administration, 100
Federal Insurance Contributions Act (FICA), 3, 4, 139
  Social Security, 3, 4
Fidelity Investments, 60
Financial advisers, 72, 166
  Certified Financial Planners (CFPs), 114; how to choose, 119; Institute of Financial Planners, 114
Fixed-income instruments, 4, 74
  asset allocation, 75; bonds, 7, 27, 29, 46–49, 51, 52, 54, 55, 75, 81, 92, 114, 116, 117, 125–127, 153, 164; diversification, 81; maturity of, 80; yield of, 76–78
401(k) plans, 2, 15, 67, 69–72, 96, 111, 141, 148, 153, 166
  asset allocation, 76, 86; borrowing from, 68, 72, 85, 88, 89, 92, 95; contributions to, 67; defined-contribution plan, 67; direct deposits in, 34; disadvantages of, 69; diversification, 78;

dollar cost averaging, 83, 85; employer contributions to, 39, 61, 67, 68, 82, 85, 86; loan collateral, 68; mistakes, 69; mutual funds, 86; number of participants in, 93; online sources, 162; rollover, 67, 95; risk, 90, 92, 94; suspending contributions, 91; switching investments, 68, 72, 86; tax advantages of, 39, 59, 61, 67, 68, 71, 72, 85, 86, 89, 90, 92, 93, 94; transferring, 94, 95; vested, 67

Fraud
    Better Business Bureau, 121; oil and gas, 121; online, 156; penny stocks, 120, 156; Ponzi schemes, 120, 156; precious metals, 120; real estate, 120, 121; Securities and Exchange Commission, 121, 161

Freelancers, 35
Futures, 51, 53

Goals, 148
Gold and silver coins, 65
Government securities, 25, 29, 52–55, 65, 81
Guaranteed investment contracts (GICs), 52

Hobbies, 28, 138

IBM, 48
Income
    calculating, 136–152; retirement, 136; tax, 153
Individual Retirement Account (IRA), 2, 61–63, 69, 70, 72, 110, 111, 115, 122, 141, 148, 153, 166
    asset allocation, 76, 122; banks, 118; borrowing from, 63, 95; brokerage firms, 11, 14, 114; changing institutions, 65; changing investments, 65; custodian, 34, 128, 129; direct deposits in, 34; diversification, 122; fees, 11, 14; history, 63; opening an account, 64; penalties, 63; rollover, 67, 95; statements, 11, 65; tax advantages, 38, 39, 59, 61, 63; trustee-to-trustee transfers, 65; withdrawals from, 63, 66, 67, 139
Inflation, 37, 70, 135, 136, 141, 143, 145
    rate, 26; real estate appreciation, 102; risk, 49, 80, 130, 131; stocks, 56; strategies to combat, 22, 27, 77, 131

Inheritances, 35
Insurance, 57, 58, 97, 114–116
    agents, 112, 116, 114, 166; auto, 103, 138, 149; banks, 116; disability, 133; health, 10, 15, 27, 57, 67, 103, 133, 138, 140, 149; homeowner's, 14, 57, 149; investments, 15, 52; IRAs, 64, 65; liability, 138; life, 57, 103–110, 138; 134, 153, 161; Metropolitan Life, 47; mutual funds, 117; online sources, 161; property, 138; salespeople, 46
Interest, 47, 81, 101
    bonds, 47, 49, 55, 56, 80, 131; certificates of deposit, 48; compounding, 33, 36, 38, 60; credit card, 39, 42, 43; fixed rate, 42; floating rate, 42; money market accounts, 52, 53; money market funds, 48, 52, 53; mortgage, 97; risk, 81, 131, 132; stocks, 56; U.S savings bonds, 29
Internal Revenue Service (IRS), 59–61
International investments, 51, 82
    currency risk, 132
Investment seminars, 81, 82
Investor Protection Trust, 4

Keogh accounts, 2, 61, 71, 148, 153, 166
    defined benefit, 71, 72; contributions to, 71; tax advantages of, 71
Keogh, Eugene, 71

Leverage, 73, 82–84, 124, 166
    online sources, 158
Liabilities, 152, 153
Life expectancies, 16, 36
Lipper Analytical Services, 128
Liquidity, 50
    certificates of deposit, 50; diversification, 78; real estate, 50, 102; short-term versus long-term investments, 51
Loans, 9, 115, 138, 140, 149
    automobile, 42, 153; bonds, 4, 7, 25, 27, 29, 46–49, 51, 52, 54–56, 64, 65, 69, 74–77, 80, 81, 84, 92, 112, 114, 116, 117, 125–127, 131, 132, 159, 164; consolidating, 39; education, 42, 149, 153; home equity, 149; refinancing, 41

Market risk, 80, 132
Market timing, 75, 132
MasterCard, 43
Maturity, 47
  bonds, 47, 55, 56, 159; fixed-income investment, 80; intermediate-term, 80; long-term,
  80; short-term, 48, 80
Merrill Lynch, 47, 60
Metropolitan Life, 47
Money market, 92
  accounts, 52; annuities, 112; funds, 48, 52, 61,
  74, 75, 131, 153
Morningstar Mutual Funds, 128
Mortgage, 9, 42, 97, 98, 149, 153
  banker, 99; FHA, 100; mortgage-backed securities, 51, 54; online sources, 159; payments,
  35; prequalifying for, 99; REITs, 98; tax
  advantages, 42
Mutual funds, 4, 16, 29, 46–49, 83, 86, 112,
114–117, 122, 123, 130, 153, 156
  asset allocation, 74; bonds, 47, 51, 52, 54, 65,
  75, 77, 80, 81, 84, 126, 127; cash, 48; debt,
  48; diversification, 48, 81, 82; dividends, 54;
  fees, 128, 129; Fidelity Investments, 60; government securities, 53; international, 82; IRAs,
  64, 65, 118; Lipper Analytical Services, 128;
  money market, 48, 52, 75; Morningstar
  Mutual Funds, 128; mortgage-backed securities, 54; online sources, 160, 162; rating,
  127–130; real estate, 57, 98; selling, 130;
  stock, 48, 51, 54, 65, 83, 126; utility, 54; *Value
  Line Investment Survey, The,* 128

National Center for Financial Education, 9
Net worth, 152, 153
  calculating, 152, 153, 163
New York Stock Exchange (NYSE), 117

Online Sources, 16, 155
  America Online, 156; annual reports, 160;
  budgets, 163; Charles Schwab, 164; Ceres
  Securities, 163; chat rooms, 158, 164; ;
  EDGAR, 160; E*TRADE Online, 164;
  Federal Trade Commission, 161; Fidelity
  Online, 162; Finance Center, 159; fraud,
  155–158, 161; investing tips, 155; insurance,
  155, 161; life insurance, 161; Merrill Lynch
  Online, 163; mutual funds, 160, 162;
  NETworth, 162; Prodigy, 156; Quicken
  Financial Network, 162; search engines, 155;
  SEC, 160, 161
Options, 51

Penny stocks
  fraud, 120, 156
Pension plans, 10, 61, 64, 67, 69–71, 96, 153
  disadvantages of, 69; retirement income, 141;
  vested, 64, 67, 70
Ponzi schemes, 120, 156
  Ponzi, Charles A., 121
Precious metals, 120
Prodigy, 156
Profit-sharing plans, 61, 70, 78, 141
Pyramid schemes, 156

Rate of return, 19, 33, 36, 43, 49, 50, 53, 54, 61,
64, 128, 130, 131, 135, 136, 144
  asset allocation, 74; average annual, 75; calculating, 71; long-term versus short-term, 51;
  mortgage-backed securities, 54; real estate, 102
Real estate, 15, 24, 57, 58, 65, 153
  agents, 98, 101; appreciation, 99, 102; buying
  a home, 97, 98; deflation, 80; fraud, 120, 121;
  investing in, 27, 47; location, 101; mortgages,
  97, 98, 153; property taxes, 42, 95, 137, 149,
  153; raw land, 51, 95; REITs, 98, 99; remodeling, 102, 103; rental, 51, 98, 148; tax advantages, 96; title insurance, 98; when to buy, 101
Risk, 130, 131
  annuities, 52; blue-chip stocks, 52; business,
  131; cash, 52; certificates of deposit, 52; checking accounts, 52; collectibles, 51; corporate
  bonds, 51; currency, 132; foreign investments,
  51, 132; futures, 51, 53; GICs, 52; inflation,
  49, 80, 130, 131; interest rate, 81, 131; junk
  bonds, 51; life insurance contracts, 52; market,
  80, 132; minimizing by diversifying, 48, 79,
  80, 124; money market accounts, 52; money
  market funds, 52; mortgage-backed securities,
  51, 54; mutual funds, 51; options, 51; raw

land, 51; rental real estate, 51; savings accounts, 52; short-term bond funds, 52; U.S. Treasury bills, 52; U.S. Treasury bonds, 52; utility stocks, 52; versus reward, 49, 51, 61, 90, 92, 130, 132, 144, 145; zero coupon bonds, 52
Rollover, 67, 95

Salary
    raises, 142; take-home, 148
Savings accounts, 12, 52
Savings and loans, 99
    Bridal Registry Accounts, 100; crisis, 28; loans, 114; money market accounts, 52; mortgages, 114; savings accounts, 114
Securities and Exchange Commission, 121, 156
    online, 160
Self-employed retirement plans [See: Keogh plans]
Shareholders, 47
Shares, 55
SIMPLE plan, 63
Single individuals, 133, 134
Social Security, 3, 4
    disability insurance, 133; Federal Insurance Contributions Act (FICA), 3; future of, 3, 4; income, 37, 50; qualifying for, 5; retirement benefits, 4, 10, 12, 23, 37, 56, 57, 141; survivor benefits, 105, 106; taxes, 136
Speculative investments, 53
    futures, 53
Spending wisely, 8, 9, 27, 32, 34, 35, 40, 41, 44, 137
    online resources, 163; savings strategies, 32, 34–36, 38, 39, 161
Stamps, 65
Standard & Poor's, 161
Stocks, 4, 7, 27, 29, 46–49, 83, 84, 114, 116, 125, 130, 131, 153
    annuities, 112; asset allocation, 74, 76; blue-chip, 52; brokers, 46, 58, 114; diversification, 79, 81; dividends, 47; exchanges, 98; IBM, 48; inflation, 56; interest rates, 56; IRAs, 65; market fluctuations, 83; market crash, 73; market timing, 76; Merrill Lynch, 47, 58; mutual funds, 47, 48, 51, 54, 65; NYSE, 117; online

sources, 159, 163, 164; prices, 56; risk, 79, 131; selling, 129, 130; shareholders, 47; shares, 55
Tax, 66, 87, 97, 123, 136, 140
    brackets, 34, 62, 86, 94; capital gains, 98; employer contributions, 61; income, 153; IRS, 59–61; lawyers, 72; loopholes, 34; penalties, 65–67, 114; on property, 42, 95, 137, 149, 153; Social Security, 136, 139; taxable investments, 94; tax-deductible accounts, 34, 40, 60; tax-deferred accounts, 2, 3, 8, 18, 19, 38, 40, 61, 63, 65, 67, 71, 76, 82, 85, 86, 90, 92, 93, 94, 111, 128, 166
Trustee-to-trustee transfers, 65

Unemployment compensation, 66
U.S. Congress, 4
U.S. savings bonds, 25
    interest rates, 29; Series EE, 29
U.S. Treasury
    bills, 52, 65; bonds, 52, 54; notes, 65

Value Line Investment Survey, The, 128
Vested, 64, 67, 68

W-2 form, 64
Wells Fargo, 47

Zero coupon bonds, 52
    IRAs, 65